STRESS BUSTING

THROUGH PERSONAL EMPOWERMENT

Authors

Thomas F. Holcomb, Ph.D.
Murray State University

George John Cheponis, Ed.D.
Growth Management Consultants

Richard J. Hazler, Ph.D.
Ohio University

Eileen McPhillips Portner, MA
Private Practice

 **ACCELERATED DEVELOPMENT INC**
Publishers
Muncie Indiana

Stess Busting through Personal Empowerment

Copyright 1994 by Accelerated Development Inc.

10 9 8 7 6 5 4 3 2 1

Printed in the United States of America

Technical Development: Cynthia Long
Marguerite Mader
Sheila Sheward

Artwork by: Shannon E. Hazler

Cover Design by: Gregory Janson

Library of Congress Cataloging-in-Publication Data

Stress busting through personal empowerment / authors, Thomas F.
Holcomb . . . [et al.].
        p.   cm.
     Includes bibliographical references and index.
     ISBN 1-55959-075-0
     1. Stress (Psychology)   2. Self-actualization (Psychology)   3. Stress management.
4. Adjustment (Psychology)   I. Holcomb, Thomas F., 1942-
BF575.S75S7725   1994
155.9'042—dc20

94-19539
CIP

LCN: 94-19539
ISBN: 1-55959-075-0

Order additional copies from

ACCELERATED DEVELOPMENT INC., *Publishers*
3808 West Kilgore Avenue
Muncie, Indiana 47304-4896
Toll Free Order Number 1-800-222-1166

TABLE OF CONTENTS

LIST OF FIGURES

CHAPTER **I**

INTRODUCTION

Stress is a fact of life. It can be frustrating, devastating, or invigorating depending on how you perceive and manage it. One thing, however, is certain: you cannot afford to ignore it. Just the fact that you have picked up this book and read the first few lines demonstrates your interest and that is an excellent first step in gaining control over stress.

WHY BE CONCERNED ABOUT STRESS?

Excessive stress has become one of the nation's leading health hazards. It takes its toll on loved ones, friends, and coworkers. It permeates our world. It is like a thief who comes in the night to rob your most valued possessions—your physical health and psychological well-being.

Thousands of books and scholarly works have been written about stress. Magazine and newspaper articles regularly warn of the problem and suggest ways of handling it. With all that has been said and written about the subject, one must question, "Why are so many people like you not doing more for their personal stress management?" Perhaps the reason lies in the fact that you have been exposed to the problem but not to your own personal solution.

Knowledge and information alone are simply not enough to ensure the successful changes necessary for you to beat stress. **Hard work, commitment,** and **personalization of problem areas** are keys to successful stress busting. This book will show you how to do the necessary work in a personalized format that will produce the understanding and commitment you need. It is similar to the time when you learned to ride a bicycle. Nobody could do it for you. They could tell you about it, help steady you, run along beside you, or even provide the aid of training wheels. But eventually you had to ride on your own. This is exactly how it is with beating and mastering negative stress. You have to get your own balance and find what works for you and your total self!

Working your way through the information and exercises in this book will help you take control of stress in your life. Once you have accepted the challenge and personal ownership of both the stress in your life and your reaction to it, you will be ready to take the action required to control stress by developing your personal empowerment skills.

Our experience as counselors and educators has convinced us that every individual can develop Personal Empowerment Skills to bust negative stress. **Personal Empowerment Skills** are the basic talents, abilities and coping strategies that everyone has at their personal disposal once they realize they are responsible and in control of their life, their behavior, and their stress. Personal Empowerment Skills encompass a holistic view of people and the integration of people's bodies, minds, and spirits into coordinated wholes. This wholistic way of being allows for uniqueness and individuality in personal adaptation and coping. This book will assist you in becoming more aware and accepting of these Personal Empowerment Skills and teach you how to harness them for your own personal betterment.

React on paper, interact with others, and then take actions based on the content and processes in this book. You are encouraged to read and respond to the book and the process more than once, because each time you do, new insights and more empowerment can be yours. Each new empowerment tool you gain will help you gain more control of your life and be a successful stress buster. The key ingredient is the fact that you do have the ability to gain mastery over areas of your life that may now be in control of you. Now is the time to take responsibility for your own stress busting through Personal Empowerment Skills development. This decision is critical to your present and future. The choice is yours and the steps needed to make your personal best choices are available in the following chapters.

HOW TO ACCOMPLISH STRESS BUSTING
THROUGH PERSONAL EMPOWERMENT

This book can be used in a variety of ways whether you are new to the task of controlling stress or someone who has been working at it for a long time. If you are a novice or have been unsuccessful in mastering stress in the past, start at the beginning of the book and work your way through the material in a systematic way. No single activity or piece of information is going to turn you from an over-stressed candidate for mental or physical problems to a calm individual who uses stress effectively. You need a well-rounded understanding of yourself, your life, and your stress that only can be fully seen through an organized approach to learning information and developing skills.

Those of you who have been studying and working with your own stress or that of others for some time will probably find your own unique ways to make the best use of this book. Your experience and study has probably already given you some degree of an overall picture of the issues and yourself. It will be up to you to determine which issues and which activities will benefit you most at your current stage of development. However, we caution you not to eliminate from your study all the information and those exercises that you have experienced before. Your previous work in the area should have convinced you that each time you study material again or do an exercise again brings new meaning and understanding. This is particularly true when you have grown significantly since the last time you actively considered the issues.

We are all full of good intentions, but good intentions alone do not eliminate bad habits, start and maintain positive behaviors, or develop new coping strategies. Energy and self-discipline are also needed and this book will show you how to make all of these work for you. There are no short-cuts or quick fixes. The price of effort is to be paid but the promise of greater feelings of personal empowerment and stress busting are the payoffs.

Take plenty of time to work through the exercises. You cannot begin taking actions that will get lasting results without first gaining insight into your thinking and feelings about your situation. Remember that you are made up of body, mind, and spirit. All of these parts must be given substantial attention if you are to gain long lasting control over your stress.

Sometimes you may find that your attempt at an exercise is getting nowhere. This is nothing to worry about since any individual exercise may not fit you at your particular stage of development. Simply move on to the next exercise. Do not cut exercises short. Give them each a thorough effort in order to get the most out of them. Try not to get discouraged when any one exercise does not make you feel much more enlightened or healthy. The accumulation of information and skills is what you are seeking and not just one major piece of information.

Get a notebook to keep with you as you experience the many activities and uncover personal information and insights. Keep a record of your personal reactions, impressions, and self-explorations. This *journaling* will provide you with insights and examples of where you are now with your stress busting and personal empowerment. It is amazing how helpful and therapeutic journaling can be. It will give you a personal history of your development which is very important as your knowledge and skills develop. You will always have stress and experience stress. The journaling you have done will let you know how far you have come and remind you of the things you may have learned but since forgotten or stopped using in healthy ways.

This is not a book to read just before going to bed each night and then not thought of again until the next evening. It is a book to help you take the actions you need to develop and practice the Personal Empowerment Skills necessary for controlling your stress. Take those actions and it will work for you.

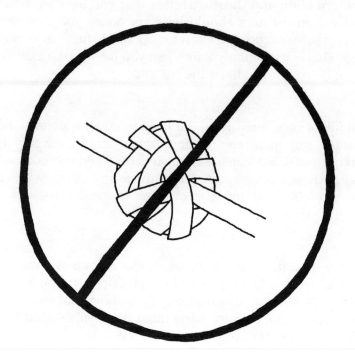

Figure 1. Undoing the knot caused by stress.

CHAPTER II

ANATOMY OF STRESS

There is little agreement on a definition for stress. This should help you understand why there are so many different approaches to dealing with stress found in book stores, newspapers, and on television. Monat and Lazarus (1977) explained that there are three general models of defining and working with stress:

1. The **Physiological** model discusses those biological and chemical reactions that take place inside the body. This model emphasizes identifying the physiological things that could go wrong or have already gone wrong and finding ways to bring them back to normal.

2. The **Psychological** model emphasizes those thoughts you have that cause you to see some daily occurrences as more of a "threat" than others. The focus in this model examines how you think or feel about things that worry you and then tries to develop more realistic ways of thinking about these worries.

3. The **Sociological** model pays most attention to the social system that surrounds you and how that system impacts your life. Material written about this model pays closest attention not to the individual, but instead to changing the environment around the person.

What are some other definitions of stress you might have been exposed to in the media? Here are a few of the more well accepted definitions. See which ones you can identify with in your life or in the life of a friend.

- Anderson (1978) — Stress is any stimulus which causes the individual to utilize adaptive behavior, which is new or different from this person's usual behavior.
- Holmes and Rahe (1967) — Stress is life changing events that serve as stimuli and lead to illness.
- Lazarus (1966) — Stress is not any one thing but it is a generic term used to cover a wide range of things.
- Selye (1974) — Stress is the nonspecific response of the body to any demand made on it.

DEFINITION OF STRESS USED IN THIS BOOK

The definition used in this book is related to all the others, but increases the emphasis on your personal human potential. It also focuses on negative stress which is what we are seeking to help you overcome.

Negative stress is an overwhelming feeling of tension, leading to physical and psychological ramifications caused by the individual's inability to develop personal empowerment skills to mediate effects of external stimuli and internal reactions.

The thing to remember is the fact that you consist of body, mind, and spirit. You must engage your total system in the stress busting process in order to achieve lasting personal empowerment development and effectively manage negative stress. This book will help you to do that. It will expand your awareness and help you look at this area in a new and different light. Remember that you must move from awareness to the taking of new and more specific actions. These specific actions will be the mediating efforts that you will be learning and that the definition above mentions.

This book will help you discover your Personal Empowerment Skills and how to use them effectively in coping and managing the negative stress in your life. *Stress busting through personal empowerment, then, is both a process and a product. The emphasis is on you becoming aware of what you are doing, taking full responsibility for your perceptions and the results you are creating, and then taking both remedial and proactive measures to change and produce more favorable results for yourself.*

MISCONCEPTIONS ABOUT STRESS

You probably have some very good ideas about what stress is because you have experienced it. Yet there are many misconceptions about what stress is as well as what it isn't.

Stress is a disease. (*Wrong.*) It is not a disease so there is no cure for it. However it does play a big role in bringing about disease.

Stress is always bad. (*Wrong.*) Stress can be good. It can be a great energizer and a wonderful motivator. This stress is positive stress and has been termed Eustress.

Stress can victimize you. (*Wrong.*) Stress is not in control when you are in control. You can allow stress to victimize you because of your perceptions, beliefs, and thinking. Therefore, it can be managed if you choose to and learn how to do so.

All stress should be removed. (*Wrong.*) Remove all stress and you might as well be dead. Excitement, joy, and just living all involve stress producing situations that make life worthwhile as well as stressful.

Stress symptoms should be treated with medication. (This is a tricky one.) Medication and medical attention is demanded for some clinical and chronic stress-related health problems. **But most stress can be managed without medication.** The causes of the stress need to be identified and the effects of stress need to be reduced by your empowerment skills.

Stress is all in your mind. (Wrong.) Stress is a response that happens inside of you. It is the price you pay for living. Since it is a real "thing," it is best managed by your talents, abilities, and unique blend of coping strategies.

Stress is the same for everyone. (Wrong.) You cause much of your own stress. Stress also gets help from aspects of life and living such as change and transitions, your expectations, needs, and relationships. Your unique perception of life's events will contribute to the degree and form of your personal stress. Your stress is different from anyone else's. Your management of stress also will be unique to you.

SIGNS AND SYMPTOMS OF STRESS

What Are Some Signs and Symptoms of Stress?

Physical:	Being tired, run down—totally exhausted, blood pressure elevated, migraines, loss of sleep or only wanting to sleep, vague aches and pains, rapid heart beat, loss of sexual desire, loss of appetite, backache, neck ache, stomach ache, and many muscle pains and spasms
Emotional:	Feeling tense, up-tight, irritable depressed, angry, self-doubt, loss of confidence, frustrated, overwrought, burned-out, short on patience, hurried-harried, worried, and just totally drown
Social:	Feeling alone, insecure, unappreciated, unsupported, lacking in confidence, lacking in control, or excessive drinking and drug abuse
Intellectual:	Cannot concentrate or think, lacking in judgment and reason, feeling bored and underutilized, pressured for time, and lacking in interest
Spiritual:	Self deprecation, lacking of purpose and goals, questioning, hopelessness, and helplessness

Actual Diseases Linked to Stress

Anderson (1978) listed the following as being directly linked to stress:

1. Cardiovascular Problems
   Coronary Artery Disease
   Hardening of the Arteries—Angina
   Hypertension
   High Blood Pressure
   Strokes
   Rhythm Disturbances of the Heart Palpitations
   Migraine Headaches

2. Muscular Problems
   Spasmodic Episodes

3. Inflammatory Joint Problems
   Arthritis

4. Upper Respiratory Problem
   Allergies

5. Infectious Diseases Problems
   Upper-respiratory Viral Disease

6. Gastrointestinal Problems
   Peptic Ulcer

7. Edocrinological Problems
   Diabetes

8. Dermatological Problems
   Eczema, Hives

9. Cancer

10. Chronic Pain

11. Immunological Disturbances

12. Genitourinary Disturbances
    Fluid Retention

13. Neurological Disease

14. Fatigue

This list clearly demonstrates that negative stress does effect the person from head to toe. It effects internal organs and the muscular-skeletal areas. It leads to diseases that can cause discomfort, disability, or even death. Stress even has an inhibiting action on the immune system that increases the likelihood of a person experiencing a great deal of stress acquiring such things as the common cold and various other infections.

What Can Be Done about Stress?

Since causes and the impact of stress are unique to each individual, stress must be dealt with differently by each person. You must learn to manage your own stress by adapting yourself and your personal environment. Take the time to find what is happening to you and then utilize your personal empowerment skills to improve your situation. Yes! . . . You can take control of your stress and your life.

Using medication alone to deal with stress symptoms or disease is simply "patching" yourself up physically. You need to make changes in your thoughts and your life-style if you want to make any lasting change. This means you are going to have to take the time to become aware of your thinking about your world and how you are choosing to live your life.

What Does Your Stress Look Like?

Directions: Your first exercise is to simply write some of your stress symptoms as you recognize them now. You can add to the list as you discover more about yourself and the things that you need to better control.

1. _____

_____

2. _____

_____

3. _____

_____

4. _____

_____

5. _____

_____

Look at the Figure on the next page and identify the physical symptoms and aspects of your stress. Look back over the symptoms you listed and put a red mark on the figure anywhere you have symptoms of stress. For example, if stress causes you headaches, you would put a red mark on the figure's head.

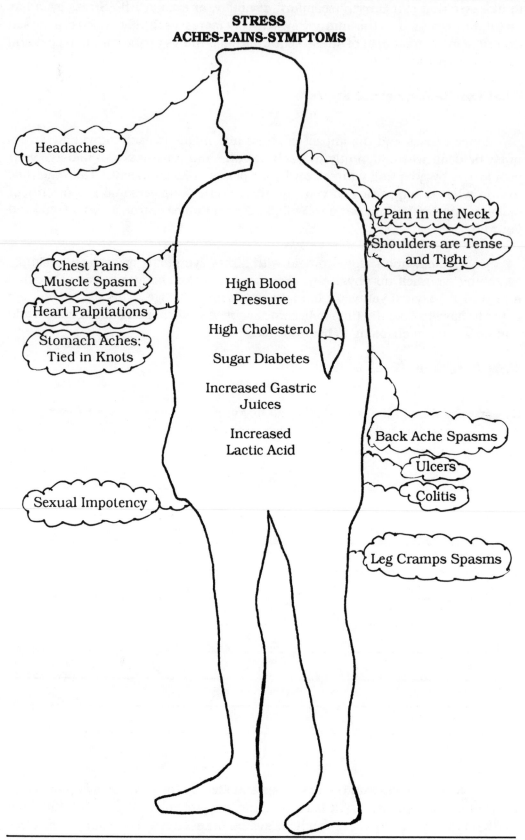

Figure 2. Places stress can physically strike the body.

THE BIOCHEMICAL PROCESS OF STRESS

How Do Symptoms of Stress Occur?

Selye (1956), a pioneer in stress work, coined the term the **General Adaptational Syndrome**. It means the nonspecific response of the body to any demand made on it that the individual perceives as a stressful situation. It is a general syndrome because any part of the body is susceptible to the effects of stress. There are three levels to this process of stress response in your body. These three levels are alert, systems ready, and fight or flight.

Level 1 — Under stress your body reacts or "goes into action." The *hypothalamus* — a part of your brain — triggers your Endocrine System. The pituitary gland produces a hormone, **ACTH**, which goes directly to the adrenal glands. The adrenal glands rush super amounts of adrenalin into your blood stream. This sets up the "flight of fight" reaction to come.

Level 2 — This alert goes out to all systems: heart, lungs, and muscles are all readied for physical action by the adrenalin pumping through your system.

Level 3 — If physical action occurs (flight or fight), it helps dissipate all these physiological preparations. If there is no release of this hyped-up physical condition, a state of emergency stays in the body. The body stays braced for action. When no action comes, eventually the system WEARS DOWN OR OUT.

Figure 3 is an example of how this might look.

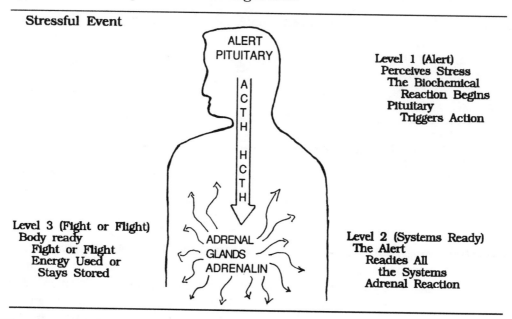

Figure 3. Three levels of stress response.

MEDIATING BIOCHEMICAL PROCESSES
WITH EMPOWERMENT SKILLS

How do these three levels relate to actual stress in your body? The alarm was triggered by you through your perception of a stressful event. Your body was then readied by the biochemical reactions going on inside.

Level 1 is the stage where your body becomes aware of perceived stress. Level 2 responds to this stress with physical and psychological preparation. Your body is reacting and getting all your systems charged up. This is the critical point for you to mediate these reactions with personal empowerment skills.

Lack of the use of personal empowerment skills at Level 2 can result in grave consequences. You can *be consumed* by stress if you do not act effectively. There is both a serious physical and mental toll on your body when you reach Level 3 if your readied system does not use this charged energy for the fight or flight response.

How you choose to act at these critical times is vitally important. You can mediate and break the traditional "flight or fight" reaction with correct reactions. This automatic response to stress was built into us to increase chances for survival. This "fight or flight" reaction that charges your body today is the same one used by our ancestors in prehistoric times. Today, however, we must translate this physical reaction into something that helps us do more than run faster or hit harder. The human mind must intervene by reducing the impact of this flight or fight reaction on the body while still recognizing that it is providing important information on our environment.

Recognizing physical symptoms is a key to stress reduction. After thinking about the information presented here, can you recall any sickness, illness, or aches and pains you have experienced that may be linked to stress and were not listed on the stress symptoms in Figure 2?

Directions: Go back now and add any more physical symptoms or problems that may involve your reactions to stress.

Additional illnesses, aches, and pains linked to your stress

1. _____

_____

2. _____

_____

3. _____

_____

Directions: Next, complete the Personal Stress Inventory (Figure 4). The Inventory will ask you to identify from a list of problems those that impact you. It will also help you to evaluate how much impact stress is having on you. After you have completed the Personal Stress Inventory of Physical Symptoms, review your list of illnesses, aches, and pains. Then, add to the list if you have identified more than were previously listed.

Personal Stress Inventory
Physical Symptoms

Evaluate your stress signs and symptoms by doing the following exercise:
1. Mark (**X**) in the left column those items which you have experienced.
2. Indicate the Frequency that you experienced these symptoms.
3. Indicate the Severity of your experience with the symptoms.

Frequency (How often does this occur?)

(**10**) 4 or more times a day; (**9**) 2-3 times a day; (**8**) once a day; (**7**) 5-6 times a week; (**6**) 2-4 times a week; (**5**) once a week; (**4**) 2-3 times a month; (**3**) once a month; (**2**) once every two months; (**1**)2-4 times a year.

Severity (How bad is it?)

(**10**) Excruciatingly severe—to—(**1**) just a trace

Experienced #	Illnesses, Aches, and Pains	Frequency	Severity
____	1. Tense muscles	____	____
____	2. Quivering stomach	____	____
____	3. Depression	____	____
____	4. Ulcers	____	____
____	5. Feeling anxious	____	____
____	6. Tight stomach muscles	____	____
____	7. Exhaustion & fatigue	____	____
____	8. Suicidal ideas	____	____
____	9. Heartburn	____	____
____	10. Insomnia	____	____
____	11. Loss of sexual desire	____	____
____	12. Arthritis	____	____
____	13. Irritable	____	____
____	14. Backaches	____	____
____	15. High blood pressure	____	____
____	16. Heart disease or irregularities	____	____
____	17. Nervous sweat	____	____
____	18. Chronic tense neck & shoulders	____	____
____	19. Diarrhea	____	____
____	20. Frequent serious accidents	____	____
____	21. Sweaty palms	____	____
____	22. Nervousness/edgy	____	____
____	23. Rage	____	____
____	24. Shallow rapid breathing	____	____
____	25. Migraine headaches	____	____
____	26. Cramps in legs or arms	____	____
____	27. Excessive eating	____	____
____	28. Intense anger	____	____

Evaluate your answers using the information on the following page (Figure 5).

Figure 4. Personal Stress Inventory of Physical Symptoms.

The following stages correspond to stress and the symptoms you checked on the preceding Personal Stress Inventory of Physical Symptoms. Circle the numbers you have checked. At each level, the symptoms become more pronounced and severe. The frequency of their occurrence will also effect how much of a real problem they are for you.

Item Number and Related Stages

Stage 1 — Risk Factors
 Item # 1 5 9 13 17 21

Stage II — Clinical Symptoms
 Item # 2 6 10 14 18 22 24 26 28

Stage III — Medical Problems
 Item # 3 7 11 15 19 23 25 27

Stage IV — Real Disease and Disability
 Item # 4 8 12 16 20

Stages and Implications

Stage 1 — Real Risk Factors
These symptoms are real signs that you are reacting to stress. The physical reactions you are experiencing at this level are still fairly mild, but they can be uncomfortable, particularly if they occur frequently.

Stage 2 — Genuine Clinical Symptoms
At this stage, your physical symptoms are getting more intense and uncomfortable. They can be quite severe and frequent although they are still manageable.

Stage 3 — Full Blown Medical Problem
At this stage, your physical symptoms have become real medical concerns and problems. You will probably seek a doctor's help with these at this time.

Stage 4 — Real Disease and Disability
Medical problems exist. These can be real and life-threatening.

Related Questions

What stage has the most checks in it for you?

Which symptoms and stages have the greatest frequency and severity?

What are the implications of that stage for you?

What do you think of the things that stress you now?

Figure 5. Self-evaluation follow-through of personal stress.

STRESS AND PERFORMANCE

The entire process of the stress response within your body can have a variety of results. One way to look at this is the effect of stress on your performance.

Figure 6 is a diagram of how stress and optimal performance are related. Experiencing too little stress or stimulation in your life will bore you with work, home life, or social life. Boredom can produce very destructive reactions, particularly related to personal or work productivity. The opposite extreme of the spectrum is too much stress. Having too much stress in your life takes a major toll on you over time and that toll is often termed "burnout." **Burnout** is the reaction to negative stress in your life that literally consumes you. Between these two extremes of stress—boredom and burnout—lies the optimum level of stress with the most positive contribution to productivity. This optimum level provides enough stress to motivate you and get you going while you are still able to manage your stress and keep it under control.

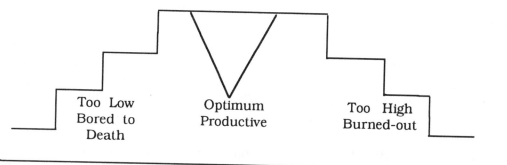

Too Low   Optimum   Too High
Bored to   Productive   Burned-out
Death

Figure 6. Performance relationship to stress.

Too little stress is not good. Too much stress brings devastating effects with time. The key is to be involved enough to engage the stress of life, but keep it within manageable limits for the optional effect on your productivity.

STRESS IN THE WORKPLACE

Opportunities, restraints, and demands are things you have to deal with every day in the workplace. Differences between that work place and your personal perceptions and values may greatly affect the expectations and needs of both yourself and your employer. When your needs, expectations, and values are not met or opportunities are not provided for them to be met, these restraints are seen as frustrating barriers. Such a situation may indeed create a stressful workplace. This is especially true if you have little control or say in the things which affect your stress level.

When wants, needs, and expectations are met by what the work environment offers, then potential stress is minimized. The larger the discrepancy between what you expect and what you actually get, the greater will be the stress and frustration.

INTERNAL AND EXTERNAL DEMANDS

Internal Demands

The pressure you place on yourself causes internal demands. These are your expectations — your shoulds, oughts, desires, and wants. These internal demands can result in major stress when they become an overreaction to actual realities. They also can bring you into conflict with what others demand from you and produce even more stress. An important accomplishment is to have a good picture of these internal stress pressures and a recognition that they are brought about by your ideas and feelings rather than the pressures of the outside world. *These you can change simply by changing yourself.* You will need to be aware of what your needs, desires, and goals really are in order to recognize and then take appropriate actions to mediate these demands.

External Demands

Things and behaviors that others (people or things) want, expect, or demand from us cause external demands. They may be related to things you do not possess or to things you do own. For example, if you own a home, it demands that you mow the grass, keep it clean, and fix things. However, not owning a home may produce the expectation in your family that one should be acquired. Another example might be at work where your boss might pressure you to attend training to learn a new skill. After you have the training, the same boss may then pressure you to take on additional responsibilities because you possess new skills. Unlike internal demands, you do not possess the total ability to control external demands. Those people and things that place the expectations upon you have considerable control over the demands. However, it is only you who can choose which demands to meet and how fully to meet them. A positive approach allows you to see that these choices are in your control even though they may often be very difficult choices with somewhat limited possibilities.

Juggling Your Total Load

One critical factor that should be obvious in each type of demand is that satisfying one demand will often lead to other demands. Recognition of this will save you from the common false assumption that, "My life will be just fine if I can just meet this one demand." Life just does not work that way. Every time you are successful in life it opens up more opportunities for yourself and others. These opportunities, whether social, personal, or professional, produce more challenges and demands.

You must add both internal and external demands together in order to get a picture of your total stress load. *Stress can be looked upon as an accumulation of many factors that could easily be handled individually but when added together they can simply be too much to handle.*

Directions: As much as possible, identify those things that you are trying to juggle at one time. List specific internal and external demands that you juggle and their impact.

Office or job issues_____

_____

Home and family concerns _____

_____

Civic efforts_____

_____

Religious _____

_____

Community_____

_____

Friends_____

_____

Stress _____

_____

Personal goals _____

_____

THE AWARENESS PROCESS
Where Are You Now?

Awareness is a necessary first step in personalizing stress. It allows you to explore yourself and your situation in order to reach a better understanding of yourself and what makes you tick. The stress scale is presented in Figure 7. Please mark your personal level of total stress in your life as given in directions.

Directions: Put a **(X)** in the place that best describes your total stress right now. Put a **(0)** in the place that best describes your general total stress level.

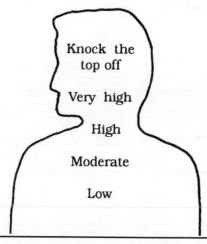

Figure 7. Stress scale—personal evaluation of present and general total stress levels.

Directions: After completing Figure 7, think back over your most recent stressful day and see if you can list things that contributed to your stress overload.

1. _____

_____

2. _____

_____

3. _____

_____

4. _____

_____

Directions: List what you consider (in order of priority) to be the greatest sources of stress in your personal life?

1. _____

_____

2. _____

_____

3. _____

_____

4. _____

_____

Directions: List what you consider (in order of priority) to be the greatest sources of stress in your work or professional life?

1. _____

_____

2. _____

_____

3. _____

_____

4. _____

_____

What are the similarities or patterns in your two lists? _____

_____

_____

What are the surprises for you on your lists? _____

_____

_____

Directions: Look back over your life. Has your stress always looked like this? One year ago? Five years ago? Ten years ago? Try to get perspective on the changes in stress levels and stress causers in your life. Record your perspectives.

_____

_____

_____

_____

_____

Personal Symptoms Summary

You should now have gained some knowledge and given some thought to stress as it relates to you. Make sure you confirm what you have learned before you proceed to the next chapter.

Personal Definition

Directions: Look back at the information in this chapter and write your personal definition of stress. What does it mean to you? What is this thing you will learn to control?

_____

_____

_____

Symptoms you can recognize in yourself

Directions: Review the symptoms of stress and list some critical symptoms that you can already see in yourself. You can look at these later to see how effective your stress busting has been.

_____

_____

_____

Stage of your personal stress

Directions: Write the stage at which most of your stress symptoms fall into._____

What is the potential impact on you of being at this stage?

_____

_____

_____

You have already begun the road to controlling your stress by learning about what you are fighting. The next chapter will provide you with information on what personal empowerment is, what it means to you, and how you can begin to gain control of it. Do not forget to make some comments in your notebook. Remember your personal reactions are important. They will tell you where you have been so you can recognize how far you go.

CHAPTER **III**

DEVELOPING PERSONAL EMPOWERMENT

What does the word empowerment mean to you? The "Star Wars" movies taught us that Jedi Warriors must learn to trust and believe in themselves and the good and powerful forces that are within them. This book is designed to give you similar insight to your own potential strengths for dealing with life and living.

> *To have personal empowerment you must trust yourself and your ability to cope and adapt to life/work demands. You must also trust and use your strengths to learn new and better self-management skills and adaptive behaviors.*

This book will help you identify those strengths available within you so that you will be able to increase your self-management skills.

Empowerment means taking personal control over aspects of your life that are sometimes out of control. For example, you can learn to lower your blood pressure, slow down your heart rate, and ease tense muscles. You can reorganize internal forces to calm harried nerves. Gaining control of these aspects of your life will then allow you to tackle work demands with renewed vigor, energy, and concentration. You also can readjust your thinking and reorganize time to allow for better management and coping. This strengthening of your total physical and psychological well being is *personal empowerment* and you are about to increase yours through working with this book.

Remember that it is up to you to make a commitment to follow through with what you learn from this book. Nothing in this book will work for you unless you work for it. Effort and persistence will make a difference.

GAINING YOUR OWN PERSONAL EMPOWERMENT

Are you beginning to understand what empowerment is?_____

Directions: Indicate how empowered you feel now by circling your level of empowerment and then state why you feel that way.

1. Greatly empowered because _____

_____

2. Empowered because _____

_____

3. Slightly empowered because _____

_____

4. No empowerment because _____

_____

5. Hope of feeling empowered because _____

_____

RETHINKING YOUR MOTIVES

It is important for you to answer some critical questions before you go much further in this book. Give the following questions some serious thought because they will help you decide how hard you are willing to work at the exercises that follow. The answers also will tell you something about how much you can expect to benefit from the exercises in the book.

Directions: Respond to the questions that follow.

1. **At the present . . .**

   a. What motivated you to learn more about stress? _____

   _____

   _____

   b. What do you desire to personally gain from this experience? _____

   _____

   _____

   c. What do you personally want to be able to do differently? _____

   _____

   _____

2. **Consider your past efforts . . .**
   a. How would you describe your **past efforts** towards actually

   doing something about the **stress** in your life? _____

   _____

b. What have you tried doing in the past about stress?_____

_____

_____

c. How would you describe your specific **accomplishments** related to

dealing with stress? _____

_____

_____

YOUR PERSONAL INTENTIONS PLUS COMMITMENT

Everyone has good intentions but good intentions are never enough to get things done by themselves. Planning, knowledge, skills, and commitment also are needed if you are to have success at anything you do.

Most of us would like to find easy answers to life's difficult questions and problems. Your ability to control stress must come from within yourself and although the answers there may be simple, they are never easy to carry out. *Busting stress through personal empowerment does require honest effort, a plan of action, hard work, integrity, and commitment*. It is no different than when you have successfully applied these same success behaviors to other aspects of your life.

Directions: Be honest with yourself. How much time, effort, and commitment have you really devoted to managing stress in your life? Check the most appropriate response for yourself.

    1. Time (How much time have you actually worked on it?)
        a. One hour a day _____
        b. One hour a week _____
        c. One hour a month _____
        d. Other (specify) _____

    2. Effort (How much effort have you really put into this?)
        a. Great amounts _____
        b. Much _____
        c. Some _____
        d. Little _____
        e. None _____

    3. Commitment
        a. Definite goals and specific written plans _____
        b. Active motivation, but nonspecific plans _____
        c. Good intentions _____
        d. Shown no active interest _____

UNDERSTANDING THE DYNAMICS OF
STRESS BUSTING BY PERSONAL EMPOWERMENT

The Stress Management Triangle (Figure 8) is a good way to think about personal empowerment especially as it relates to acquiring stress busting skills. The components of the Triangle are Process, Commitment, and Review.

Process implies that you must spend time looking and examining the various aspects of yourself and your life. You must take your own personal inventory and become aware of the specific aspects of stress in your life. You will be doing that in the next chapter.

Commitment is at the focal point of empowerment. Without commitment, you will not be able to dedicate yourself to the necessary efforts nor have the drive to follow through with purposeful behavior. Action gets results. The power of purpose helps produce the results you want.

Review is the need to examine your progress and how your plans and goals are working. This leads you back to the processing component and keeps the eternal triangle of growth and renewal in motion.

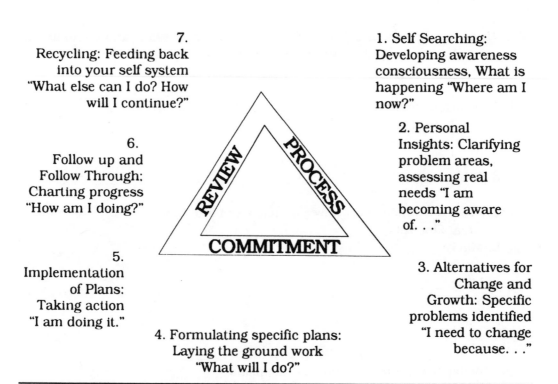

7.
Recycling: Feeding back into your self system "What else can I do? How will I continue?"

6.
Follow up and Follow Through: Charting progress "How am I doing?"

5.
Implementation of Plans: Taking action "I am doing it."

4. Formulating specific plans: Laying the ground work "What will I do?"

1. Self Searching: Developing awareness consciousness, What is happening "Where am I now?"

2. Personal Insights: Clarifying problem areas, assessing real needs "I am becoming aware of. . ."

3. Alternatives for Change and Growth: Specific problems identified "I need to change because. . ."

Figure 8. Stress management triangle.

USING THE STRESS MANAGEMENT TRIANGLE

The stress management triangle (Figure 8) provides a means to understand how one learns and uses personal empowerment skills. It gives a picture of the ways and means of the process in general but not for the specifics of your individual case. The outline on this page can be used in many circumstances where you wish to implement the stress management triangle to further develop your skills.

Directions: Feel free to use the outline now or at any time in the future to help connect the theory to your personal situation.

1. Review
    How are you going to review your progress?

    a. _____

    _____

    b. _____

    _____

    c. _____

    _____

2. Process
    What have you learned about yourself?

    a. I learned . . . _____

    _____

    b. I became aware . . . _____

    _____

    c. I relearned . . . _____

    _____

    d. I have insight . . . _____

    _____

3. Commitment
    What will you commit to do differently based on what you have learned about yourself, stress, and your personal empowerment skills?

    a. _____

    _____

    b. _____

    _____

c. _____

_____

d. _____

_____

THE SELF-GROWTH PROCESS OF EMPOWERMENT

You have already involved yourself in the process component of our model by reading and participating in the activities included thus far in the book. You are off to a good start. More self-exploration lies ahead in very specific areas that will further increase your understanding and ability to take action to improve your empowerment skills and your life.

Your involvement to this point should have clarified the types of things you will be doing. You will be asked some thought-provoking questions that do take time and effort to answer. The work also takes integrity. The effort to put forth honest self-exploration and self-assessment is vital for personal empowerment to be developed and stress busting skills to be ingrained.

Stress busting through personal empowerment begins with self-exploration. It will involve and stimulate you to new growth and great heights of self-development only after you have processed where you are, who you are, and what you are doing. Then, and only then, can relevant plans of action be specifically created, personally designed, and effectively implemented.

Your empowerment skills are the key to personal stress busting. No one can tell you how to live your life or provide easy answers to life's challenging questions. Stress is a fact of life and your life will be lived as effectively and creatively as your unique personal strengths and empowerment skills will allow!

You may have already changed your view of yourself and this self-growth process of busting negative stress through personal empowerment. These changes are very important to recognize and the process by which you give them recognition is called *reviewing* and *recycling* your ideas and information.

Recycle Your Needs

Directions: To help you understand how you recycle your needs, answer the following questions.

1. What do I want most out from this experience? _____

_____

2. What successes have I had in the past in understanding and
managing my negative stress?_____

_____

_____

3. How much energy have I put behind my past good intentions? _____

_____

_____

4. What do I need to do differently?_____

_____

_____

CHAPTER IV

CONTROLLING YOUR WORLD

Stress comes from many sources in everyone's life. Home, work, health, family, friends, and business associates all play unique roles in a person's stress load. Have you ever stopped to pinpoint your troublesome stress sources? See Figure 9. Do you know when your stress load turns into an overload or real distress?

Directions: Answer the following questions as you look at Figure 9.

When have you felt like this? _____

_____

_____

Where does this happen to you? _____

_____

_____

When does this happen to you? _____

_____

_____

Why does it happen to you? _____

_____

_____

_____

What might it take to get control back

for yourself?_____

_____

Figure 9. Who is pulling the strings?

ANOTHER VIEW OF YOUR WORLD

Stress is in all aspects of your life, but it does not always come from the people and factors outside of you. People have a role in manufacturing their own stress. Try to find out where and how you produce your own stress.

We do not all see life in the same way. Everyone has his/her own unique perception of life. The perceptions you have of life have a great affect on what you feel and how you respond to things. These perceptions of the events in your life are results of all your experiences. It is important to explore broad aspects of your life and how you live so you can have a personal perspective and bring your stressors into clearer focus. Understanding your personal perspective of stressors also will tell you more about your role in creating and continuing them.

Directions: Respond to the following items so as to gain a better understanding of your own personal perspectives on life.

1. **Personal Perspectives** (How do I really see myself and my world?)

    a. Right now I see my world as . . . . _____

    _____

    _____

    b. Right now I believe my life . . . . _____

    _____

    _____

    c. Right now my future . . . . _____

    _____

    _____

2. Were your comments positive, negative, or neutral? _____ Why are they like that? _____

    _____

    _____

3. How have your perceptions of your life changed over the years?

    _____

    _____

4. How, if any, is your view different than how you think others perceive the world?

    _____

    _____

5. What would it take to change your view of your world?_____

_____

_____

EXTERNAL SUPPORT SYSTEMS

Zest for life and living is greatly affected by stress. Personal stresses can get in the way of your hopes and dreams. External support systems can soften these stressors and improve your perceptions of life and your morale. You must be supportive of yourself, but you need the support of others also.

Questions such as the following need to be considered. What are your external support systems? How do you seek and use the support of others? How much emotional support do you feel you actually received in your personal life and your work life?

Directions: Mark **(P)** at the place on the line below that describes the amount of support you receive from those in your personal life.

Mark **(W)** at the place on the line below that describes the amount of support you receive from those in your work life.

None   Little   Some   Average   Above Average   Way Above Average

Directions: Now break down the emotional support you get into specific aspects of your life.

What do you receive from . . .   What are you **not** now getting that would help?

Family_____   _____

_____   _____

_____   _____

Boss or Authority Figure _____   _____

_____   _____

_____   _____

Friends or Peers_____   _____

_____   _____

_____   _____

INTERNAL SUPPORT SYSTEMS

You need support systems inside you (internal) to provide purpose and meaning for your motivation. Motivation is a key to dynamic living as long as it is based on personal needs and not confused with what others need, want, and desire of you. Let yourself become aware of your wants. Abandon the "shoulds," "oughts," and "musts" that you incorporate from others. These thoughts are subtle forms of entrapment that stand between you and your personal fulfillment. They can box you into a bad career and a dull life if you let them.

What are the intrinsic rewards in your life? These are the ones that match your internal purpose in life and give you the most personal satisfaction. How much internal support and reinforcement do you give to yourself?

Directions: Mark **(P)** at the place on the line below that describes the amount of support you receive from yourself in your personal life.

Mark **(W)** at the place on the line below that describes the amount of support you receive from yourself in your work life.

None	Little	Some	Average	Above Average	Way Above Average

Directions: Now break down the reasons you have for doing things into specific categories. Write the reasons and purposes you provide to yourself for doing each of the following:

The ones I do for the significant others in my life _____

_____

The ones I do for my personal goals _____

_____

The ones I do for my personal growth and creativity _____

_____

The ones I do for my spiritual benefit _____

_____

The ones I do to gain experience _____

_____

The ones I do for my future _____

_____

The ones I do but do not know why I do them (These may need the

most attention, if they cause problems) _____

_____

PERSONAL EXPECTATIONS OF LIFE

Expectations are critical aspects of hope. Hope adds to life and also helps you as a form of support. This support strengthens your internal motivators. Understanding your personal expectations and making sure they are realistic are therefore important ingredients in determining your ability to deal with life and its difficult decisions.

The next two activities are designed to help you analyze your expectations of life and living.

Directions: Mark **(P)** at the place on the line below that describes the level of expectations you have for your personal life.

Mark **(W)** at the place on the line below that describes the level of expectations you have for your work life.

None   Little   Some   Average   Above Average   Way Above Average

Directions: Write your answers to the following questions.

1. What are some of your specific expectations for yourself? _____ _____

_____

_____

2. What are some of your expectations for your family? _____

_____

_____

3. What are some of your expectations about your place of work? _____

_____

_____

4. What has disappointed you or has not met your expectations at home or work? _____

_____

5. What opportunities or hopes do you have of meeting your expectations? ___

_____

6. What impact do the expectations you listed currently have on you? _____

_____

_____

LIFE'S HURTS AND FORGIVENESS

Another area that will impact your empowerment program for change is your attitude towards life's hurts and disappointments. What long-time hurts or grudges might you be harboring? Life's hurts and bruised feelings can contribute to angry, negative, or cynical feelings. Stress compounds these negative feelings and they in turn increase the negative stress in your life.

Forgiveness is an important component for dealing effectively with these hurts or disappointments. Can you forgive yourself for taking or putting up with so much or for being so sensitive? Can you forgive others for what you believe they did to you or for their lack of attention? Forgiveness allows for second chances at fixing the things that have gone wrong. Second chances release stress because one mistake will no longer ruin everything. These second chances are critical in an imperfect world with imperfect people. We DO make mistakes, some of which are very big. Forgiveness provides us with the opportunity to recognize human fallibility in others and to provide them with another chance.

What hurts have you collected over the years that make forgiving hard?

_____

_____

_____

_____

_____

_____

Who could you work to forgive that would allow another chance for a better

relationship and less stress on you?_____

Remember that you are seeking empowerment which requires that you let go of some of this old baggage. New productive ways of thinking and acting can then take the place of these unproductive thoughts and feelings. Dr. Hans Selye, father of modern day stress research and an internationally famous scientist, was asked what could a person really do to reduce his/her stress. This man of science simply said, "Work to earn thy neighbor's love." Forgive, forget, and use the resulting energy to move yourself forward.

Everybody has been hurt and disappointed at different times in life. It is important to identify these hurts and become more aware of them and the stress that they may be adding to your life. You cannot eliminate hurts, but by recognizing them you can learn to deal with their effects on you and on others.

1. DISAPPOINTMENTS

List things in your life that have disappointed you, that are related directly to you as well as those related to other people or other things in the world (car, job, etc.).

_____

_____

_____

_____

2. PROMISES BROKEN OR EXPECTATIONS NOT MET

a. What expectations have others conveyed to you that have not been met?

_____

_____

_____

_____

b. What expectations have you conveyed to yourself that you have not met?

_____

_____

_____

_____

3. RELATED BEHAVIORS

a. What are you doing to keep these feelings alive in you or to let them go?

_____

_____

_____

_____

b. How much energy and stress do these hurts and disappointments add

to your life? _____

_____

_____

_____

c. How are hurts and disappointments pulling your strings and controlling you? _____

_____

_____

_____

d. What human prices are you paying for not letting these go? _____

_____

_____

_____

_____

TIME AND STRESS

Time and your ability to manage it effectively is strongly related to stress. However, stress is not directly related to how much time you actually have. In fact, how you feel about time is as important as how you actually use it and both are more related to stress than the amount of time actually available.

What are your general feelings about time? _____

_____

_____

Do you always feel hurried? _____

Do you have lots of time on you hands or only a few minutes for yourself? ___

_____

Time is a stress factor because it must be managed effectively for you to feel good about its use and the time it takes to produce results. Expectations about what you truly need to accomplish also must be addressed.

Important Daily Tasks

What key things must you accomplish each day?

1. _____

2. _____

3. _____

4. _____

5. _____

Setting Your Personal Priorities

Many things might be accomplished in a day, but your priorities are the ones you give the most commitment because you value them above other things. Setting and acting on priorities should help you control the use of time in your life. You should be spending time on the priorities you set for yourself since they are most important.

List your most important personal priorities.

1. _____

2. _____

3. _____

4. _____

How Do You Spend Your Time?

Below is a time bar. It represents one day or 24 hours. Imagine that this bar could be broken into 24 one hour segments. Think about what you normally do during a day and break this bar up into segments that apply to how you spend time. For example, you might section 1/3 of the bar as work time and another 1/3 as sleep and rest.

Directions: Try to section off areas such as these and others—watching T. V., eating, hobbies, etc..

_____

0 Hours   24 Hours

How well do your priorities show up in your use of time?

Try to break general areas down even further on the additional bars shown below. For example, what are the specific ways you spend your time at work? Try to break this general time down into specific time segments. A teacher, for example, might have something like this—5 hours actual teaching, 1 hour at school preparing, 1 hour at home preparing, 1/2 hour grading papers, 1/2 hour dealing with paper work and tracking student progress.

_____

0 Hours   (At home time)   _____ Hours

_____

0 Hours   (Work time)   _____ Hours

_____

0 Hours   (Recreation time)   _____ Hours

0 Hours	(Weekend time)	_____ Hours
0 Hours	(_____ time)	_____ Hours
0 Hours	(_____ time)	_____ Hours
0 Hours	(_____ time)	_____ Hours

ACCOMPLISHMENT BLOCKERS

What are those things that block you from accomplishing what you want? What things stand in the way of using your time for the real priorities in your life? Being blocked from your goals or priorities produces frustrations and stress over which you can gain control.

Directions: Identify your greatest blocks to effective use of your time by listing your mild distraction blocks and real hindrances.

1. **Mild Distraction Blocks** (These can get you off course as inconveniences.)

a. _____

b. _____

c. _____

2. **Real Hindrances** (These are major frustrations that really get you worked up.)

a. _____

b. _____

c. _____

REVIEWING THE CONTROLS IN YOUR WORLD

Now is the time to look back over what you have identified as the controls on your life, your priorities, and how you are spending your time. Sometimes the things that give you the most satisfaction are things you give little attention. These are the situations that lead to extensive stress when they are allowed to continue. On the other hand, spending time on your real priorities, utilizing your support systems, and taking control of your life will reduce stress to healthy levels.

Directions: Review what you have done so far in this book and complete the following.

1. I realize now that most direction in my life has come from _____

_____

_____

_____

2. The internal and external means available to me to get support for myself

and my life are _____

_____

_____

_____

3. The most important things I learned about my time and priorities are _____

_____

_____

_____

4. The things that seem to block my effective use of time are_____

_____

_____

_____

5. Based upon what I have learned thus far, it seems I will need to_____

_____

_____

_____

CHAPTER **V**

EMPOWERMENT BALANCE SHEET

To think about the specific sources of empowerment in your life is important before you can fully identify the personal actions needed to control your stress. Taking inventory is a practice no retail business can do without. It is required to manage resources in ways that will lead to success. The same is true regarding the taking of a personal empowerment inventory. You must be aware of your strengths and resources and how they can work for you before you begin to take effective actions on a consistent basis.

Awareness and understanding of available resources is particularly critical as it relates to managing stress. Only through awareness and understanding will the utilization of your special empowerment skills be possible. This section will help you take a closer look at you empowerment inventory through the five areas of personal resources (Figure 10).

Figure 10. Self shelf of five areas of personal resources.

IDENTIFYING YOUR EMPOWERMENT RESOURCES
WHAT YOU HAVE GOING FOR YOU

Directions: Place **(P)** at the point on the line that describes your personal resources.
Write in specific strengths or problem areas below the line.

1. **Physical**
   (energy, strength, fitness, nutrition, etc.)

   Low_____ High

   _____

2. **Emotional**
   (self-confidence, areas of comfort, feeling of being in control)

   Low_____ High

   _____

3. **Intellectual**
   (creativity, humor, concentration, insight)

   Low_____ High

   _____

4. **Social Support**
   (friends, family, ability to reach out to people)

   Low_____ High

   _____

5. **Spiritual**
   (faith, values, commitments, goals, purpose)

   Low_____ High

   _____

QUALITY CONTROL

The degree to which you believe you have some control in your life and career
is important.

Directions: Rate yourself on the following scale to get a clearer picture of the type
and degree of control you have in your life.

Circle the way you feel about yourself based upon the following scale:
   (0) Out of my control
   (1) I have little control

(2) I have some control
(3) I have lots of control
(4) I have total control.

1. My daily energy level	0	1	2	3	4
2. My satisfaction with my accomplishments	0	1	2	3	4
3. My daily moods	0	1	2	3	4
4. My daily worries	0	1	2	3	4
5. My feelings	0	1	2	3	4
6. Change	0	1	2	3	4
7. Career or personal growth	0	1	2	3	4

The fact is that you really do have control over all seven areas of your life. No one but you can control these areas for you. Take control of these areas and you will greatly increase your self-empowerment.

PERSONALITY STYLES
SAFETY VERSUS RISK TAKING

Your personality also effects how you respond to situations and how you meet your needs. **Needs** are drives or desires that influence what motivates you. Remember how you prioritized your needs when you looked at your own personal purposes and goals? This time you will look at the ways you go after those goals.

Risks are an inherent fact of life. Risk nothing and you receive nothing. However, if you are always out on a limb taking grave risks, then you are in a high stress situation both physically and emotionally. Security feels nice for awhile, but placing too much energy into being safe and secure will lessen your ability to take any risks. Consequently, this leads to a very dull life. This kind of security is not helpful.

Directions: Identify the term below that best describes you.
Place **(P)** at the place on each line that best describes you in most situations. Make notes to remind yourself of why you answered the ways you did.

Risk Taker _____ Security

Racehorse _____ Leisure Pacer

Challenger _____ Compliant

No Control of Life _____Total Control of Life

Always racing and risking is not good for you and going too slowly is not much better. Both extremes are too stressful for body and mind. Pacing your time, energy and needs is vitally important so that you can be just as productive in 10, 20, 30, or 40 years as you are now.

Taking up the challenges of life is a good quality for effective pacing. *Challenging* life is similar to being on a positive offensive and looking for opportunities. This enables you to have effective control in your life because you are ready to act when the time is right. *Control of your life is yours as long as you recognize the choices to be made.* You can change directions and responses to become a challenging self-paced person in control of your life plans. The choice is yours.

PERSONAL STRENGTH
REFOCUSING ATTENTION ON YOURSELF

Directions: Make a list of all the strengths you personally possess. If you think you are friendly, intelligent, caring, etc.—write it down. Try to be objective. Picture yourself as an objective observer. What would an objective observer say about you?

My Strengths

_____

_____

_____

_____

_____

_____

Directions: To gather more data about yourself, ask a couple of good friends or your spouse to make a list of some of your most positive traits (emphasize positive traits only). This will help you get an even more accurate picture of yourself. Write them down.

How others see my strengths

_____

_____

_____

_____

_____

_____

Directions: Use the center of the target (Figure 11) to place all the strengths that you identified in yourself that were also identified by others. These indicate how your perception of yourself agrees with how others see you. These will be highly productive strengths in your life. They will bring you many benefits.

Use the outer edge of the target to write the other strengths seen by yourself or others but not both. These are hidden strengths that are recognized by some people but not everyone. They may bring you benefits but they will never be fully useful or appreciated since they are not uniformly recognized. Why are these not seen by everyone? Why don't you and others both recognize them?

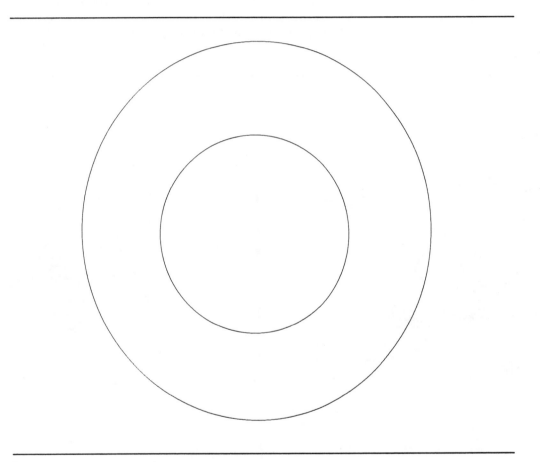

Figure 11. My personal strengths target.

You perceive certain personal strengths but nobody else sees them. Perhaps you can work on making these hidden strengths more visible so that others can recognize and see them more readily. If others said you have certain strengths but you do not see them in yourself, ask yourself why not? You obviously exhibit these positive behaviors and demonstrate them, so why do you not recognize them? Perhaps you do recognize them, but will not give yourself credit. Why might that be? Believe in yourself and free yourself to enjoy all your personal assets.

BALANCING THE SCALES

You have spent time looking at both the inhibiting aspects of your life as well as positive personal resources. Now is the time to ask, "How well do they balance?" Do the positive aspects of your life and personality equalize or outweigh your stressors? It is important to put this information into a realistic perspective.

Most of the time people tend to focus their attention on what they do not have going for them. For example, say a person had 80% of their potential and strength developed, but they chose to focus their time and attention on the 20% they had not developed. The scales would be way out of balance! Think about this. It is very important for you to put yourself into perspective. Do you have a balanced picture of your life or are you giving too much attention to one side?

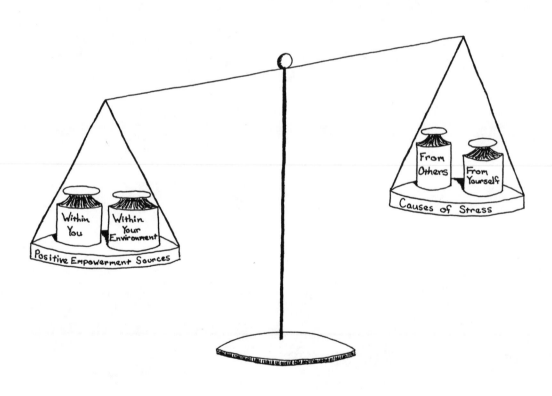

Figure 12. Balancing the scale with positive empowerment sources on one side and causes of stress on the other side.

Directions: Using Figure 12 as an example, list those things that would go on each side of the balance.

1. What are the positive empowerment sources within you?

_____

_____

_____

2. What are the positive empowerment sources within your environment?

_____

_____

_____

3. What are causes of stress you have from others?

_____

_____

_____

4. What are causes of stress you give to yourself?

_____

_____

_____

REFRAMING YOUR BALANCE

The previous exercise asked you to examine the balance of the positive and negative forces operating in your life. If you believe that your scale came out on the positive side, then you have acknowledged that you do have the personal empowerment resources already operating in your life. You simply must put more emphasis and attention on what you have going for you. You must keep these strengths and supports uppermost in your mind and use them consistently. These are the assets that will help you plan strategies for coping and managing life's challenges.

Another important procedure is to reframe experiences in life as "life's challenges" instead of life's problems. Challenges help you think about managing and coping instead of resisting and avoiding. Challenges activate problem solving strategies rather than negative responses.

If you still feel that your resources are much lower than the stresses and negative aspects of your life, it may be time to reframe them as challenges. This may be the time when a professional counselor can help you. It is normal for everyone to need the help of others in dealing with life's challenges at some time or other. Unfortunately, many people do not think about using this opportunity and suffer needlessly. Professional counselors can help you reexamine life's demands in ways that are supportive of the person you are and the one you can become. They can help you use the personal empowerment skills that are definitely available to you.

The choice as to what you will do is up to you. But you do have a choice! It is time again to stop and reconsider what you have learned in this chapter.

Directions: Complete the following statements in ways that help you to reconstruct what you have learned and what it means to you.

1. I learned . . . . . _____

_____

_____

_____

2. I relearned . . . . _____

_____

_____

_____

3. What I have going for me that I am most pleased about . . . . _____

_____

_____

_____

4. What I need to work on is/are. . . . _____

_____

_____

_____

_____

CHAPTER VI

EMPOWERING YOUR SYSTEM

No one else is like you. You are capable of thinking, feeling, setting priorities, and acting on specific commitments and goals. Your physical, emotional, intellectual, social, and spiritual aspects combine to make you a total system. Integrating these different aspects into a *well balanced* and evenly paced life activates your personal empowerment system. *This total personal empowerment system is greater than the sum of its individual parts.* It draws its energy from maintaining balance and keeping all the systems functioning at an optimal level. Neglect one aspect of your total self and other aspects of your self-system will be weakened and more vulnerable to the stress and strains of harried life-styles.

Work for your empowerment by first accepting *who you are* and *what you are capable of accomplishing in five dynamic areas of your life.* Combat the crises of negative stress by utilizing these areas and seek wholeness through your greatest asset — your *empowerment system* (Figure 13).

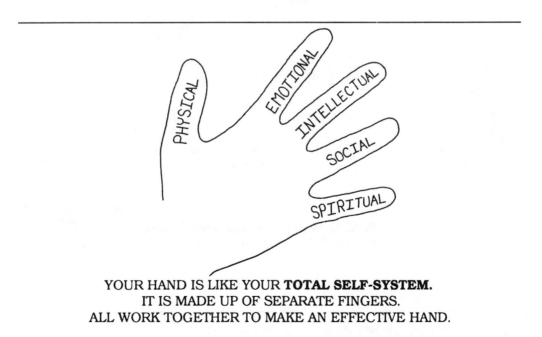

YOUR HAND IS LIKE YOUR **TOTAL SELF-SYSTEM.**
IT IS MADE UP OF SEPARATE FINGERS.
ALL WORK TOGETHER TO MAKE AN EFFECTIVE HAND.

Figure 13. Hand representation of five dynamic areas to form your total self-system.

BALANCING AND PACING

Think of yourself and your life as a tightrope walker. It is full of excitement and challenge! It has risk and rewards! But it also takes practice and skills to make everything work. When you demonstrate commitment to coping with the continuous challenges that are presented, you can get it all done.

Imagine yourself now as a tightrope walker. You use your "balancing pole of life" consisting of your five systems working in harmony to keep yourself under control and balanced. Think about how the excitement, challenge, and balance apply to your life. Figure 14 is an illustration of balancing and out-of-balance. Look at all you have to cope and manage continuously. What are the skills and practice you need for success?

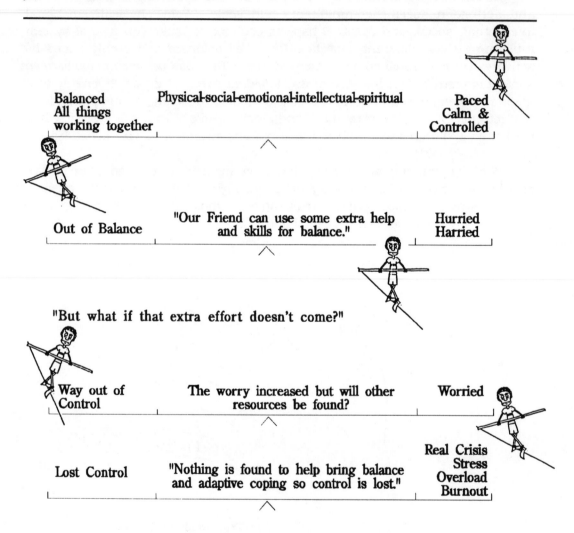

Figure 14. Illustration of balancing and out-of-balance.

The rest of this chapter will show you how to find the skills necessary to keep your balance in life. Just like any professional tightrope walker, some times will be scary. There will be challenges which will require the tightrope walker in you to keep things steady and get refocused before moving on. Coping and mastering life's challenge does require practice and the development of greater skills and strategies. You can do it!

STRESS BUSTING STRATEGIES

Many specific techniques will be presented in this chapter to help you obtain and maintain a balanced perspective for your life-style. Empowerment is enhanced by practicing stress busters. Three types of categories of stress busting strategies are provided to assist you.

The *strategies* you will be learning *are the means of marshalling and concentrating your forces in coordinated ways.* By utilizing the right personal skills, you can cope and manage difficult aspects of your life, including the management of negative stress, more effectively.

Prevention Strategies

Prevention of stress focuses on your unique life-style. Prevention is the proactive use of personal stress busters such as being in good physical shape, having a variety of social supports, viable goals, and a life of purpose. Prevention allows you to work for total fitness and wellness in all aspects of your life. It takes a sincere commitment to wellness to effectively utilize this strategy. It is an attitude and way of life.

Mediation Strategies

Mediation implies that you must activate certain strategies at critical times. These strategies are short term relievers of stress and revivers of your energy. They will empower you during difficult times. They will help you maintain or reestablish balance when you feel yourself getting out of control. Or they may simply give you that little extra boost we all need at times.

Remediation Strategies

Remediation, as used here, implies intervention during problem times. Emergency intervention is demanded when you cannot handle the battle alone. Chronic out-of-control stress can develop a crippling hold on you. Professional attention is needed when emotional or physical ailments develop into real health problems or concerns. Professional assistance includes the use of counselors, psychologists, psychiatrists, and physicians.

Summary of Strategies

These three types of strategies are summarized in Figure 15. Prevention and mediation are strategies you can use without outside help. Remediation is a strategy where you seek outside help from professionals because you need assistance in coping with and managing the negative stress of your life.

Strategies Used Independently	PREVENTION Wellness promotes helping yourself with a total orientation to healthy living
	MEDIATION Techniques to help yourself disrupt or lesson the stress response
Strategies Needing Outside Help	REMEDIATION Chronic health problems Professional help as needed

Figure 15. Summary of three types of strategies.

PHYSICAL EMPOWERMENTS

Physical exercise is an excellent prevention tool for controlling stress. Exercise builds your body so that you can operate at greater efficiency. Increased efficiency then helps you to withstand the demands that stress places on you physiologically. Getting your body in good shape and keeping it that way is a great prevention strategy for empowering yourself.

Exercise is also a great way to mediate stress by working off the stress that builds up in the body as tense muscles, headache, and other body pains. Finishing a workout also increases relaxation as the body regroups and the natural chemicals and physiological reactions associated with physical exercise and recovery work for you. It also helps build up your immune system.

Walking, jogging, cycling, and swimming are all methods of exercise that promote stress reduction. Keep in mind these few tips as you begin your planning for physical exercise.

1. See your physician. Get a physical to be certain of the best possible health plan for you.
2. Start slowly. If you begin too strenuously, your muscles will hurt more than necessary and you will be more likely to quit prior to any benefits. Pay attention to your body.
3. Set aside a regular exercise time. This encourages exercise as a habit rather than a rare event.
4. Be social. Exercise with friends to build a social support system as well as a physical one. Accomplish two things at once whenever comfortably possible.
5. Use the right type of footwear. Your feet are important to comfort and wellness, so treat them well.

Remember the old adage of *sound body and sound mind*? There is lots of truth in it since you are a "total" system. Physical Empowerment can be both a prevention and mediation strategy. You only have one body. It is important to take care of it and exercise it wisely so it will continue to serve you well.

Directions: Take time to consider answers to the following questions.

1. How much exercise do you get on a regular basis?

   _____

   _____

2. How did you feel and look the last time you had a regular exercise pattern?

   _____

   _____

3. What first steps might you take to start a new and better physical empowerment program for yourself?

   _____

   _____

NUTRITIONAL EMPOWERMENT

How you treat your body nutritionally is very important to empowerment. A well-balanced diet is a necessity for your physical self and a major factor in how well your total self is in balance. Nutrition can be both a preventive and mediation strategy. It also can be something with which you are forced to deal because of serious problems that should have been taken care of earlier.

The "Coffee Break" Cycle

During breaks in your routine what do you do? Drink soda or coffee and eat junk food? This may hype you up for an instant instead of regenerating you for the long-run. The caffeine in coffee and soda can add to your stress. Do yourself a favor when your stress gets high. Eat a healthy snack such as fruit, vegetables, nuts, or some juice and use the caffeine and sugars as isolated treats rather than necessities.

The Sweets Cycle

High sugar content in food is simply not good for you. This goes for sweetened soft drinks too. Yes, sugar might provide an immediate high, but you will pay for it dearly when your energy level drops soon afterward. If you keep this up, it could even send you on a roller coaster with sugar highs and lows that will make you feel out of control.

Artificial Colors, Additives, and Preservatives

Chemicals, Chemicals, Chemicals! Read the labels of what you are consuming. Artificial colors, additives, and preservatives can all have a negative impact on your mind and body. Try this simple experiment. See if you notice the difference in yourself after you eat certain products which have large amounts of additives in them. Learn what additives effect you most, then try to find healthier foods for yourself.

A Better Nutritional Pattern

Put yourself on high octane fuel. High energy equals good nutrition. Your body needs high fiber and low fats. They contribute to being "heart smart" and add up to a longer life for many people.

Water

Also make sure you drink lots of water. Water is very important since it cleanses the system and provides needed moisture to all body parts.

Directions: Make a list of all you eat and drink in a typical day and for the weekend. Then examine what the list looks like? What would be quality changes you could make?

Weekday	Ate and Drank	Quality Changes
Breakfast		
Lunch		
Dinner		
Late Evening		

Weekend
Saturday Breakfast		
Lunch		
Dinner		
Late Evening		

Sunday Breakfast

_____

Lunch

_____

Diner

_____

Late Evening

_____

PSYCHOLOGICAL HARDINESS
EMOTIONAL AND SPIRITUAL PREVENTION STRATEGIES

Preventative measures exist regarding your emotional and spiritual well-being as well as those for your physical self. Kabosa (1979) found three such factors which helped individuals "hang tough" in difficult times (commitment, control, and challenge).

Commitment

Committing yourself to what you do helps meet the demands of your personal and work life. It comes from acting on the values and goals you hold most dear. The less commitment you demonstrate, the more stress takes control. Commitment provides the purpose to keep you focused and gives you personal meaning.

Control

Gaining control is the feeling you have when you decide what you do as well as how you choose to think and respond. The feeling of control gives us a realistic hope that anything is possible. Without feelings of control and hope, we are easily discouraged. Effective actions are generally taken when feelings of control and hope are present.

Challenge

Facing life and its issues as a challenge helps you view change as a fact of life that should be approached rather than avoided. You can choose change and embrace the challenge of the new and different. Accepting change and treating life as a challenge will raise your excitement level about life. It is amazing how simply recognizing new demands as challenges rather than disasters will effect your ability to function effectively as a problem-solver. Your life will look very different depending on whether you respond to life as a challenge or as a problem!

Hardiness Factors

Commitment, control, and challenge can be considered hardiness factors. They are your attitudes about life and living. Demands, pressures, and responsibilities are strenuous aspects of life that you can deal with more easily when you empower yourself with these hardiness factors. Commit yourself, challenge yourself, and believe you can exert control over situations and you vitalize powerful positive prevention strategies that will produce positive results. It is like being a tough minded optimist who knows he or she can manage and cope with life demands and expect mastery over life's challenges!

MEDIATION STRATEGIES

You can take specific actions to help mediate the effects of stress in difficult situations. Most of these actions involve some means of extracting yourself from the stressful situation both physically and emotionally for a limited period of time and in a controlled manner. They are designed to use all aspects of your body, mind, and spirit to overcome the potentially overwhelming feelings of tension that can develop through negative stress.

Relaxation Break

Taking a relaxation break is the most common general example of how to regain control of your stress during difficult times. A relaxation break primarily consists of using one of many relaxation methods to calm yourself down, regroup your energy, and refocus your thinking. By taking a relaxation break, you can literally take yourself away from the stressful situation in a controlled manner. This breaks the cycle or the stressful state and allows you to again deal with the same issues, but with less negative stress to distract you.

The point is simple but can have profound effects and produce very productive results. You simply stop the treadmill from running by letting go of everything and literally getting away from it for a short period of time. This relaxation break allows you to regain a clear focus. Your "treadmill running" mind is allowed to be calmed so that it can refocus on the work at hand. By letting go and relaxing, you are putting everything out of your mind. This break renews your spirit and allows you to regain a more productive style of functioning.

Remember from the earlier discussion about stress that it is important to break (or mediate) the fight/flight response associated with stress. Look at the "treadmill running" example in Figure 16. The "treadmill" reaction state must be interrupted. You can do this and regroup your forces and concentration.

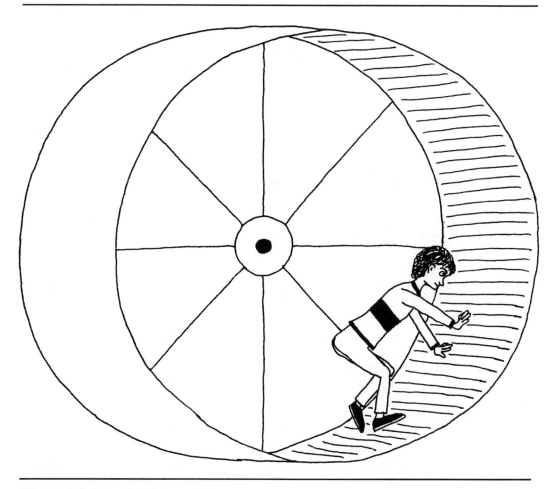

Figure 16. Treadmill running.

KEEPING TRACK OF YOUR STRESS AND
YOUR PROGRESS AT CONTROLLING IT

Maintain awareness of how well you are interrupting or mediating your stress. An objective scale should be helpful in both measuring your current success and your progress. The scales on the following page can help you to recognize even slight differences and will be particularly helpful when you are working on relaxation exercises.

Take a subjective reading of your stress level each time you work on one of the mediating exercises. For example, a time when you felt maximum stress would rate 100% and a time when you felt no stress would be 0. Make an evaluation of where your stress level would be within this continuum. Making such judgments on a regular basis will help you to recognize both problem times and success at dealing with stress. Taking readings before you try mediating strategies and after you have completed them will also demonstrate the personal power you have to control your own stress.

Use a similar evaluation scale to evaluate your relaxation levels every time you use a mediating exercise. This will be helpful in making you aware of slight changes in your relaxation levels. These small changes can make a large difference in you over time and recognizing them will increase your confidence in the progress you are making.

Keep a record of these readings so that you will see your continuing improvement and control over your stress. Closely watching your growth will be very reinforcing and it will help you learn to pay closer attention to your body, mind, and spirit. The closer attention you pay to these aspects of yourself, the more successful you will be at controlling them.

Directions: Use the following to keep a record of your stress level and relaxation level after mediating exercises. Two scales are provided. Make more copies for your record.

1. Situation causing stress _____

Stress Level before Relaxation
0% _____ 25%_____ 50% _____ 75%_____ 100%

Relaxation Level after Mediating Exercise
0% _____ 25%_____ 50%_____ 75%_____ 100%

2. Situation causing stress _____

Stress Level before Relaxation
0% _____ 25%_____ 50%_____ 75% _____ 100%

Relaxation Level after Mediating Exercise
0% _____ 25%_____ 50%_____ 75% _____ 100%

The Meditation Process

Meditation is a wonderful tool for helping people relax. Certain forms of meditation have strong eastern cultural and religious ramifications. However, meditation in its simplest form increases your concentration and helps your mind and body recover. By concentrating on a specific word or object in a planned manner you can take your mind off yourself and your present circumstances. The end result is a relaxed condition and a calming process.

Benson (*Relaxation Response*, 1975) discussed various forms of meditation. No matter what form is used, the results seem to be the same. Taking time to quiet yourself and become reflective allows your inner self to relax. You take control of your state of consciousness which is clearly a form of self-empowerment.

Benson (1975) identified four main ingredients for developing an effective relaxation response: (1) quiet environment, (2) an object to dwell on, (3) a passive attitude, and (4) a comfortable position.

Directions:

1. Practice the meditation process.
2. Find a nice quiet place where you are free from distractions.
   Close the door to the room. You may even use ear plugs.
3. Sit comfortably in a chair with your eyes closed.
   Relax all your muscles. Just drop your shoulders and let go.
4. Concentrate on something: Focus on an object or an extremely calming scene.
   Continuously repeat a word or hum a song or poem line.
   Refocus your attention if you stray.
   Don't force yourself. Just gently let this happen.

You are trying to attain a passive inner state which will result in a quieting and calming response. Your attention is on something other than daily circumstances. Practice several times a day for 5-20 minutes. Maybe you are like this.....

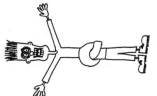

tied up in knots

You get your attention off of your stresses and daily grueling routine and change the knots to this.....

tranquility

It takes practice to learn to relax effectively. Do not get upset if it does not go well at first. Just keep a passive attitude and you will experience the relaxation response in time. Remember, you cannot hurry up to slow down. Just let go and allow time and practice to work. These results will be worth the effort.

Deep Breathing

Deep breathing is another effective mediation strategy. Various ways and techniques exist to accomplish this so do not expect the technique that works for your best friend to be also the best one for you.

What type of a breather are you? Put one hand on your chest and one on your stomach. Take a few natural breaths. Do you breath through your abdominal-stomach area or are you a thoracic-chest breather? It is better to be a stomach breather as this allows for much deeper, more relaxed, and rhythmic breathing. This will be the area to focus on as you do the following techniques.

Directions:

1. Practice deep breathing relaxation.
2. Sit comfortably in a quiet room.
3. Breathe in through your nose to the count of three and make sure you fill up your abdominal cavity.
4. Exhale out your mouth to the count of five.
5. Repeat this process 3 or 4 times for practice and to see initial effects. The more comfortable you become with this technique the more widespread stress reduction and relaxation you will realize.

Directions:

1. Reenergizing yourself with your eyes closed.
2. Picture a bright white light above your head. Feel the warmth on your head as you take in a breath. Feel the energy and warmth move from your head, down into your shoulders, and to your chest.
3. As this warmth and energy fills your entire body, picture the pressure and tension moving down and out through your toes.
4. Feel this energy and warmth move down your body to your stomach and buttocks as the pressure and tension moves out.
5. Now feel the warmth and energy move down to your toes and to fill your entire body.
6. Feel the power and energy you are gaining.
7. Now count up to five and snap your finger to be alert and reenergized.

Try combining deep breathing with some imagery, and or meditation for reenergizing yourself. Experiment a little to find the best type of results that you can produce.

Systematic Relaxation Procedures

To be relaxed and uptight at the same time is physiologically impossible. Learning to relax is your way of telling your body to let go of the pressures and uptight feelings and tensions. You probably have more control over your body than you now realize and certainly more than is normally used. The following exercise will teach you to relax by contracting (tightening) and loosening (letting go) muscles while sitting comfortably in a quiet place.

Directions:

1. Start by closing your eyes and then concentrate on taking nice, deep, easy breaths.
2. Focus your attention on your right hand and arm.
3. Make a fist with your hand and a muscle in the upper part of your arm. Notice the pressure and strain and the energy it takes.
4. Now let go of this tension as you count down from 5 - 4 - 3 - 2 - 1 and 0. Just let yourself go. . . relax. Let your hand and arm fall to your side and give yourself permission to relax. . . . .
5. Now try the same thing with your left arm and hand.
6. Follow the flow of tension and pressure leaving your arms and hands.
7. Notice the difference between feeling the pressure and feeling it gone.

Directions:

1. Relax the head and face by using systematic relaxation procedures.
2. Focus attention on your head. Wrinkle up your forehead, scrunch up your nose, clench your teeth, and push on the roof of your mouth with your tongue.
3. Notice the uncomfortableness and the energy it takes.
4. Now let go as you count down from 5 - 4 - 3 - 2 - 1 and 0. Just let yourself go and tell yourself to relax.
5. Feel your forehead smooth out as the pressure and tension rolls down your cheek and away.
6. Give yourself permission to relax.
7. Refocus your attention on your face again and concentrate on all the little muscles around your eyes, your mouth, and jaw.
8. Tighten them and then let them relax also.

Directions:

1. Relax your neck and shoulders.
2. Focus on your neck and shoulders.
3. Lean your neck back and scrunch up your shoulders.
4. Notice how quickly the pressure and tension builds up in this area.
5. Shake out your shoulders, and feel the pressure and tension move down your neck, out through your shoulders, and away as you count down from 5 - 4 - 3 - 2 - 1 and 0.
6. Give yourself permission to relax completely.
7. Focus your attention on your neck and shoulders again and this time picture any pressure or tension in your neck and shoulders. This particular tension often feels like knots.
8. As you again count down from 5, visualize all those knots loosening up and falling away as the pressure and tension leaves this area of your body.

Directions:

1. Relax the chest and stomach.
2. Fold your arms over your chest and push from the outside as you take a breath and then push from the inside.
3. Feel the pressure and tension build up quickly across your chest.
4. Now exhale, take a nice, deep breath and let your arms fall loosely to your sides.
5. Each time you count down from five while you exhale, feel more and more of the pressure and tension leave your body.
6. Refocus your attention on all of the muscles in your chest area and just let them relax.
7. Next suck in your stomach and tighten it up.
8. Notice how uncomfortable this is and the energy it takes.
9. Let your stomach relax as you count down from 5.
10. Feel more and more of the pressure and tension leave your stomach area.
11. Refocus on all the stomach muscles and let them relax.

Directions:

1. Relax the lower body including your legs and feet.
2. Raise your right leg and bend your right ankle just enough to feel pressure and tension.

3. Let your leg fall slowly as you count down from 5.
4. Feel the pressure run down your leg and out through your toes and away.
5. Now focus on all the muscles up the back of your leg and thigh and let these muscles relax as well.
6. Focus your attention on the buttocks, hips, and the small of the back.
7. Tighten the buttocks and arch your back to feel the pressure and tension.
8. As you count down from 5, let the pressure and tension go from this part of your body as well.

Directions:
1. Do a full body relaxation.
2. Concentrate on relaxing your entire body by visualizing that your body is a sand bag.
3. As you count down from 5, visualize all the pressure and tension draining out and piling up outside of you like sand out of a sand bag.
4. Add a pleasant scene for greater relaxation. Now that you have relaxed most parts of your body, picture yourself at a scene that is only yours to enjoy. It might be the ocean, a lake, the mountains, or the woods.
5. Picture this scene vividly with yourself enjoying this scene and relaxing even more deeply as you also feel the relaxation.
6. Notice the wind on your face and the sound of the birds.
7. Become aware of the sun and its warmth.
8. Stay with these feelings of complete relaxation for a few minutes and enjoy your own private island of peace and tranquility. It is yours to return to whenever you need it. Visit it often.

Relax. . . Unwind. . . Feel calm, warm, and relaxed. Using a countdown also helps condition your relaxation to this process. As your skills increase you will be able to relax quickly by just counting down from five and telling yourself to just *let yourself go.*

Having a special relaxation scene also can add and enhance your ability to relax. You condition a relaxed state by the picturing of this scene, so make sure you practice this part as well as the muscle relaxation.

Practice also will help you to tell the differences between being "tense and uptight" and relaxed. You will be able to stop your tense feelings on the spot as they begin to occur. There is genuine personal empowerment in this and it is yours for the taking.

RECENTERING FOR WINNING CONCENTRATION

Yes, you can increase your concentration power. You can do it when you choose because you are now becoming the one in control. You can acquire the energy to do whatever task you need to do at home, work, or school. The steps that follow will give you strategies to use for reviving your ability to concentrate.

Directions:
1. Relax and let yourself go.
2. Breath deeply.
3. Turn the palms of your hand up to help create a passive state.
4. Smile a big smile.
5. Let your smile grow big and take over you as you let go of tension, frustration, and other treadmill running symptoms.
6. Now, close your eyes and visualize yourself doing the task.
7. Smile again with the sensation of accomplishing the task.
8. As you are concentrating, break large tasks down into small steps that you can visualize.
9. See yourself accomplishing each small task.

Relaxation and attention are mutually supportive. By relaxing and letting go of tension, you can regain energy and attention to the task at hand. This works because you are abandoning the distractors that make you less productive.

Relaxation is important to your concentration because you concentrate with your entire physical and mental being. Energy is needed to maintain tense muscles. Loosen up and you will have more energy available to concentrate. Let go and regroup to regain control. It really is up to you, and you can do it.

ASSERT THYSELF

Positive assertiveness skills are demanded in many situations. Learning to regularly stand up for what you believe, in positive ways, is critical to leading a life that feels successful and one that keeps negative stress to a minimum. This sounds simple, but people very commonly have trouble doing it with certain people or in certain situations.

The most common assertiveness issue related to negative stress levels is learning to assert yourself effectively when you disagree and/or to turn down requests which are not in keeping with your values. It is natural to want to be supportive of others but when this is done to the continuous detriment of one's own needs, it becomes a major problem for everyone concerned. You must learn to say "no" comfortably in order to make your "yes" answers meaningful. If you do not assert yourself when you feel you should, negative feelings and becoming overburdened can turn to resentment of others and a loss of control of your life. When these go unchecked, they add up to major stress.

Many opportunities occur in the normal day to practice being assertive, but many people need to have a little more structure to start. You also should look for ways to practice where the end consequences are not too great. If lacking assertiveness has been a problem for you in the past, you should not expect to make all the right moves immediately. It will take practice.

You can try this practical exercise as a way to practice saying "no" more effectively.

Directions: Have a friend read the following directions for you to follow:
1. Pick up one chair and hold it.
2. Also hold three books.
3. While holding the chair and three books, pick up and hold another chair.
4. Add three more books.
5. Add paper and pens.
6. Add four more books.
7. Keep adding things until you refuse to take any more OR until you have to ask for help.
8. Start over and we will repeat the process a second and third time.

You should have recognized the frustration in this exercise as you tried to follow directions that simply became impossible. There was no way out other than giving up or asking for help. This process physically demonstrates what we call "overload." **Overload**—whether physical, mental, or emotional—leads directly to negative stress. By controlling overloads you can immediately reduce stress and control burnout. Remember, it is your right to say NO and to ASK FOR HELP.

Directions: Answer the following questions.
1. What have you learned about your ability to assert yourself?

_____

_____

_____

2. When, where, and with whom are you most likely to allow overloads to occur? Why?

_____

_____

_____

3. What can you do to improve your ability to assert yourself and avoid overloads?

_____

_____

_____

QUICK PHYSICAL DE-STRESSORS

Many times just learning to "let go" of our pressure and tension on a regular basis can be very helpful in keeping stress from becoming distress. The following DE-stressing exercises, if practiced routinely, will help. Try them all to find the ones that work best for you in the situations where you need them. The real key to controlling distress is to create your own personal solution through your unique empowerment skills.

Directions for Exercise Entitled "Push me-Pull me"
1. Place the base of the palm of your right hand on the base on the palm of your left hand.
2. Take a breath and push vigorously to the count of three.
3. Exhale and let your arms drop to your lap.
4. Lock the tips of your finger on your right hand over the tips of the fingers of your left hand.
5. Breathe in and pull to the count of three.
6. Then take a big deep breath and just let yourself go.
7. Repeat this process and note how it brings an immediate lessening of pressure and tension.
8. Respond to the following two questions:
   a. How did this one work for you?
   b. What results did you have?

Directions for Exercise Entitled "The Puppet on a String Release"
1. Recognize that sighing can be very beneficial.
2. Stand up and imagine that you are a puppet on a string. There are strings on your arms, heads, and legs.
3. Now sigh. . . . and as you do, let your arms and shoulders become as limp as possible; just like someone let go of your strings.
4. Repeat the sigh response and this time let your neck and head fall forward becoming as limp as possible.
5. Sigh again, and this time imagine all your strings being let go. Double over as far as is comfortable to become limp and relaxed, giving yourself permission to just let go.
6. Repeat the series again until all the strings are gone and you feel relaxed.
7. Respond to the following two questions.
   a. How well did this exercise fit you and your needs?

   _____

   _____

   b. When might you use it?

   _____

   _____

Directions for Exercise Entitled, "Back DE-Stressors"
1. Do sit ups—The best cure for your back is to strengthen your stomach.
2. Do sit ups with legs bent to strengthen these muscles. Your back will love it in the long run if you do not overdue it.
3. Do the Back Rocker—Lie down on your back on the floor. Bend your knees. Gently hold them bent while rocking back and forth.
4. Answer the following questions:

a. Could you feel immediate relief?

b. What will the long-term and short-term benefits of these be for you?

Directions for Exercise Entitled, "Neck and Shoulder DE-Stressors"
1. Lock your fingers together and raise them over your head to the back of your neck.
2. Keep your elbows in and gently lean your neck back to stretch it. Do not strain; just gently stretch.
3. Repeat several times. Shrug your shoulders several times and let loose to finish.
5. Recognize that these may help at work or when you must concentrate for long periods.
6. Answer the following question, "What were your results?"

Directions for Exercise Entitled, "Head Massage"
1. Recognize that headaches are very common with stress and tension and that a gentle rubbing of the temples will help.
2. Massage the entire temple area and imagine that you are at a warm, soft, favorite spot.
3. Imagine the warmth throughout your body and just let yourself relax as you continue to massage your temples.
4. Realize that this exercise is not likely to eliminate all headache symptoms but it should help all tension headaches.

Look for the particular massage techniques that work best for you.

Become aware of the places where stress physically effects you most and you can gain some control of it with exercises similar to the ones mentioned above. Try all the exercises first to see which ones fit your needs and style best.

QUICK MENTAL DE-STRESSORS

Your imagination can have many healing qualities if you take the time and energy to learn to use it more effectively. The following exercises can help you reduce stress as you find the ones that work best for you.

Directions for Exercise Entitled "The Five Minute Vacation"
1. Realize this is a short-term vacation.
2. Recall your scene from previous relaxation exercises? With practice, you should be able to see and feel yourself there or other places whenever you want. Your mind will actually not recognize many of the differences between real and imaginary if you use your imagination well.
3. Go to the Bahamas, enjoy the peace and beauty of a woodland, or relax at a concert.
4. Learn to have several places you can go to renew your spirits.
5. Answer the following question, "Where are the best places for you to go on your five minute vacation?"

Directions for Exercise Entitled "Spring Cleaning & Cleansing"
1. Imagine that your mind has been closed up all winter long.
2. See yourself letting in the bright fresh spring day.
3. Let your eyes and ears be the windows to your closed mind.
4. See and smell the fresh spring day coming inside.
5. Feel the breeze and bright freshness and allow for a good airing.
6. Enjoy the fresh invigorating feeling.
7. Come back revived.
8. Answer the question, "How good does it feel to imagine this fresh start?"

Directions for Exercise Entitled "Internal Screaming"
1. Picture yourself in a huge canyon away from everybody.
2. Now watch yourself lift your neck and let out one great yell starting from the pit of your stomach.
3. Feel and hear the blood curdling scream.
4. Listen to it echo down the canyon and move away to nothing.
5. Feel the release as all the pent up frustration and tension leaves your body with this monster scream.
6. Repeat as needed or until you are screamed out and physically drained.
7. Try to get in touch with how great it feels to just let it all out in a giant yell?
8. Try an alternative for this exercise by finding yourself an actual place away from everyone and give a real yell.
9. Answer the question, "What adaptations of this work best for you?"

SELF-TALK AFFIRMATIONS

Did you know that people talk to themselves all the time? They do. You are in constant communication with yourself and you can choose to make those communications positive or negative. Self-empowerment and lowered stress levels require honest self-talk with an emphasis on the positive. The trick in controlling this self-talk is to focus your attention on the productive events happening around you.

Take control of your self-talk because many things are happening in your daily life, and you cannot focus on all of them at once. For example, you might be going to the bank to cash a bonus check, when you turn your ankle on the bank door step. Do you congratulate yourself on the bonus check and enjoy the treat you will buy with it? Or do you chastise yourself and hobble quickly from the bank because of your sore ankle and the embarrassment of tripping on your way into the bank? You have the choice to talk to yourself about the good things in your life or the negative ones. It should be pretty clear that emphasizing the positive ones and deemphasizing the negative ones will lead to a calmer and more pleasant existence.

Remember that your body is preprogrammed for the fight or flight response to tense situations. Your adrenalin will flow and emotions (positive and negative) will soar at tense times. It is up to you to talk to yourself and take control of the thought processes that are directing your body. You can remain calm and handle things by affirming your strengths and not dwelling on the negatives.

You can mediate your responses by positive self-talk. One way to prepare yourself is to develop some basic affirmations that you can use often enough that they become second nature to you in difficult situations. Many of these can come out of the personal strengths list you developed earlier. The following are some general ones that most people can use in one form or another.

"I am calm and in control . . . I can handle it!"

"I have the skills to manage this . . . I am in control!"

"I can cope with these challenges . . . I have the skills!"

"I have the strength to hang in there . . . I can take the challenge!"

"I am good . . . and I can get through this!"

HA! HA! HA! HA! HA! HA! HA! HA!

Laughter and humor are fantastic medicine and mediators. Try to develop your humor by seeing the lighter side of life. Learn to laugh at yourself and how seriously you take this imperfect world and your imperfect self.

Laughter is a great release, but using it can take practice. Work at taking a brief smile break if laughing out loud does not come easy. Smiling allows you to stop and let go . . . of physical and mental pressures. Try on your smiling face on a regular basis. This is another free technique with many benefits.

Empower yourself with a smile!!!!

Be on the lookout for things that make you laugh. Collect them, show them to others, and bring them out periodically to enjoy. It may be a cartoon strip, a picture, a memory, a short article, or a joke that does it for you. Just remember to keep handy whatever things make you laugh so you can get to them. Try using them on a daily basis.

Directions: Answer the following two questions:

1. What are the effects hearty laughter has on you?

_____

_____

2. What are the best ways for you to make laughter occur?

_____

_____

REMEDIATION FOR CHRONIC STRESS PROBLEMS

When you have tried and adapted all the techniques and are still stressed-out, you may need remedial help. Remedial help simply means you cannot do sufficient stress management on your own at this time. We all have such times!

Look up a counselor or psychologist in the yellow pages of the phone book. Talk with more than one about how they work and whether your issues seem to match their style of work. They are helpful because of their professional training, their ability to see us in a more objective light, and their ability to adapt general techniques to our specific situations.

You also might consider biofeedback training. This is where you are hooked up to a machine that helps your mind and body more quickly recognize your physical reactions and to make physical adjustments.

Choosing a remediation strategy and getting outside help before problems become crippling are wise choices. Everyone needs help along the journey of life at some time. It is the wisest of us who recognizes the need and actively seeks the necessary help. Treat the costs of this choice as an investment in yourself just as you would invest in a mechanic to work on your car's problems to make it run better and last longer.

PERSONAL EMPOWERMENT SKILLS NOTEBOOK

You will not improve your stress level just by reading the exercises in this chapter. You must practice. The greater number of exercises you try and the more often you do them, the stronger will be your personal empowerment system. It is important to remember which skills you have developed, which work best for you, and which need more work. Use the *Personal Empowerment Development Activity Form*, shown on the next page, to start a personal empowerment skills notebook that follows the development of your newfound skills.

Fill out a form each time you try a new activity. Keep the completed forms together and you will begin to see a clear picture of how you are helping yourself and the ways that work best. Over time this will develop into a natural plan of action that will inspire confidence in your stress fighting ability. Your notebook also will offer opportunities to go beyond the material presented in this book, since there are many other materials that will add depth and breath to your personal empowerment system.

Copy as many forms as you need or write out your own forms in your Empowerment Journal.

Personal Empowerment Development Activity Form *

Activity _____

Purpose _____

Date, time, & place done _____

Stress rating _____   Before_____%   After_____%
Relaxation rating _____   Before_____%   After_____%

What I got from the activity _____

_____

_____

What could I do differently to improve results? _____

_____

_____

_____

*Permission is given to reproduce this form for personal use.

Personal Empowerment Development Activity Form *

Activity _____

Purpose _____

Date, time, & place done _____

Stress rating_____   Before_____%   After_____%

Relaxation rating_____   Before_____%   After_____%

What I got from the activity _____

_____

_____

What could I do differently to improve results? _____

_____

_____

_____

*Permission is given to reproduce this form for personal use.

CHAPTER **VII**

TAKING ACTIONS TOWARDS LIFE-STYLE REORGANIZATION

A big part of making positive changes in the way you manage stress includes taking the actions needed to reorganize your life-style. This book should have helped you understand some of the actions you need to take. Now the ability to recognize the need, organize an action plan, and take action rests with you. Decisions must be made as to what actions to take and which ones deserve higher priorities in your situation. The end product is to fully equip yourself with personal empowerment through a variety of changes.

Examine the various aspects of your life. Picture yourself watching a large T.V. screen with a movie on about your life and your stress. Try to evaluate yourself as an objective observer. How does the story go? What will you have to do to develop a happier ending? Write down those things about your thoughts and behaviors that need the most work.

Things I need to start or revive: _____

_____

Things I need to stop: _____

_____

Things I need to ignore: _____

_____

Things I need to put in a different perspective: _____

_____

_____

Things I need to smile or laugh about more often: _____

_____

_____

Things I really enjoy and need to do more often: _____

_____

Things for which I need to be thankful: _____

_____

Things I value and on which I should spend more time: _____

_____

_____

You should now be recognizing how the actions you take will effect the management of your stress. What would the impact be if you take these actions?

_____

_____

REFLECTIONS

You can often get new insights and understandings by looking in just a little different way at something with which you are familiar. Much of the information and exercises included in this book are designed to help you do just that. Review what you have learned about yourself from this workbook experience and the ways you look at yourself differently.

_____

I have learned . . . . _____

_____

_____

I now understand . . . . _____

_____

_____

I rediscovered that . . . . _____

_____

_____

I relearned that . . . . _____

_____

_____

What three things will you absolutely commit to do differently based upon what you have learned?

1. _____

_____

2._____

_____

3._____

_____

Directions for Exercise Entitled "Telling My Commitment"
1. Tell someone what things you will do.
2. Force yourself to state your commitments as specific as you can.
3. Share those commitments with another person. By doing so your commitments become much more powerful. Who is/are the person(s) you will tell?
4. Identify the person or persons with whom you will share your commitment.

a. _____

b. _____

c. _____

Directions: List three ways by which you will keep track of your improvement.
1. _____

_____

2. _____

_____

3. _____

_____

CHANGE
BALANCING SECURITY WITH RISK-TAKING

Facing change and making changes are hard for people to do. This is true even for those who seek and enjoy change. The conflict is that people seek the same stability that change threatens. People also die from stagnation, and risk-taking is needed to overcome this state. Everyone is then in a position where they both fear and demand change in some form in their lives. With our finances, we attempt to save (security) at the same time we invest or spend (risk-taking) the money in an attempt to produce a "better" life (change). We do much the same with our energy and emotions. We try to keep emotions within ourselves most of the time (security) while we know that we must let them out (risk-taking) in order to make life better for ourselves (change).

We are seekers of change, but also creatures of habit. Many times we keep repeating the same self-defeating behaviors and feel bad about them. We continue to choose these habits rather than working out another strategy or trying another way. We are often easily discouraged and afraid to the point that we do not try or we give up too easily.

Balance has been a word used frequently in this book because it is easy to lose sight of balance as you work on change. Be ready to give both sides of yourself the attention they need. You will need to do some things to create a degree of safety in a world with some consistency. But you also need to accept the risks involved with seeking necessary growth and change in your life. **Balance is the goal!**

What are your needs for security that are most critical?_____

_____

_____

What changes do you most need to make in your thoughts, emotions, and

actions?_____

_____

_____

What are the risks involved in making your important changes? _____

_____

_____

What security behaviors will balance the risk-taking you need to take?

Security Behaviors	Risk-taking Behaviors
1. _____	1._____
_____	_____
_____	_____
2. _____	2._____
_____	_____
_____	_____
3. _____	3._____
_____	_____
_____	_____

SMALL EFFECTIVE STEPS
VERSUS
HUGE KILLER STEPS

A thorough evaluation of your need for positive change can lead to much larger tasks than you had expected. These big change tasks must be broken down into more manageable steps. Small steps that can be successfully accomplished are what is needed. Many different ways exist to attack a problem when you know specifically what you are trying to accomplish. These smaller steps will make these tasks more achievable and you more comfortable.

The following experiment will give you an idea of the benefits of the small step approach to your big tasks.

Directions for Exercise Entitled, "Recognizing Benefits of the Small Step Approach."

1. Do the Huge Killer Steps
   a. Go to a big steep hill.
   b. From your position at the bottom of the hill, look all the way to the top. The top of the hill represents your goal.
   c. Capture thoughts running through your thinking, e.g., "It looks steep. I'll bet it'll be difficult. Will I make it?"
   d. Start walking or running as fast as possible to get to the top quickly. Keep looking at how far you are from the top. (Don't hurt yourself!)
   e. Reflect on your feelings and thoughts along the way.

2. Do the Small Successful Steps
   (Approach the same experiment a second time in an entirely different manner. This time you are going to use the small steps method.)
   a. Go to the same big hill.
   b. This time, look only in front of you about four feet. Concentrate on something like a mark in the sand or a piece of dirt.
   c. As you reach this first spot, flash your eyes ahead another four feet and concentrate on this new goal. Continue this pattern all the way up the hill by always concentrating on the spot four to five feet ahead.
   e. Reflect on your feelings and thoughts along the way.

3. Now compare the two approaches
   a. Compare your feelings, thoughts, and success using the Small Step method to those experiences using Huge Killer steps.
   b. Recognize that the larger the task, the more you need the Small Step method to find success. A big job broken down into small jobs makes a good job!
   c. Answer the question, "Which of your big tasks, could benefit from this Small Step method?"

A SMALL STEP EXAMPLE

The following outline plus the Specific Action Plan on the next page will help you see how effective decisions, setting priorities and the small step-by-step method can be used to obtain goals and empowerment skills presented in this book for overcoming stress.

Directions: Write your response to each of the following six questions.

1. Identify one thing in your life where you would really like to show improvement. Try choosing something from one of the important self-system areas presented previously (physical self, social self, emotional self, intellectual self, and spiritual self).

   _____

2. What could you do to make just one small improvement in this area? Alternatives:

   a._____

   b._____

   c._____

   d._____

3. What are the physical and emotional costs of doing these?

   a._____

   b._____

4. What would you need to give up? _____

   _____

5. What would you gain from taking these actions? _____

   _____

6. What might be a good balance for you between costs and gains?_____

   _____

   _____

MY SPECIFIC ACTION PLAN *

You must state what you will do in behavioral terms (actions that can be seen and counted).

I will _____(behavior)

for _____(amount of frequency) for _____(specific time)

by _____(specific date).

> For example: practice *systematic relaxation* (the specific behavior) for *20 minutes* over *three consecutive days* (specific duration or time).

My last step to accomplish this goal is to _____

_____

> For example: My last step to accomplish this goal is to *actually do the relaxation during the prescribed time.*

My first step to accomplish this goal is _____

_____

_____

> For example: My first step to accomplish this goal is planning *where and when to do it.*

Other planning steps include_____

_____

_____

> For example: Other planning steps include making *arrangements for the kids to leave me alone and for my spouse to answer the phone if it rings.*

Plan with as many details as possible so that you will have the greatest possible chance to successfully follow through with your Small Steps Plan.

_____

* Permission is given to reproduce this page for personal use.

SELF-CONTRACT *
A SPECIFIC PLAN OF ACTION

The proof of personal empowerment is in the results that you create. This is the time to put those good intentions of stress busting to work by making a contract with yourself to take specific action.

Statement of the Particulars

I (your name) _____

will (specific plan of action) _____

_____

_____

_____

_____

I will judge my progress based on _____

_____

_____

_____

I (signature) _____ commit myself to this action.

Date_____

Witness #1 _____

Witness # _____

_____

*Permission is given to reproduce this page for personal use.

PEER PARTNERSHIP CONTRACT *

Contracts are commitments. Allowing others involvement in your commitment greatly increases its power and the likelihood of accomplishing the task. This peer partnership contract identifies the investment of another in your efforts.

I (partner's name) _____, have agreed to check with _____ regarding how he/she is doing on work towards his/her goal. I have read and understood the specific plan of action (behavior, time, and frequency).

As a partner checker, I will be as supportive as possible, and I will be sure to discuss the following as a minimum:

1. What are you doing to meet your goals (what went well or poorly)?

2. What are you gaining from your efforts?

3. How important does your goal continue to be? Is it still good or does it need specific changes?

4. What do you specifically want to happen next and why?

5. What is your next move?

Explain the specific steps you will take for your next plan of action?

Last Step to Goal (List this one first)

First Step

Other Steps

I have read and understand the specific change program described. I will discuss it with you periodically and help you check on your progress as I see it.

Peer Partner signature _____ Date _____

Dates of progress checks _____ _____ _____ _____ _____

_____

*Permission is given to reproduce this page for personal use.

FINAL COMMENTS

Modern technologies abound in all phases of our lives. Higher levels of personal empowerment technology also exist within you to beat stress. You can lower your blood pressure and relax tense muscles through relaxation training. You can release helpful endorphins into your body and be healthier through physical exercise. You can restructure your thinking and control responses to present life situations and future emotional upsets. You can use imagery and self-talk to program your mind to successfully manage difficult situations. You can be healthier by working for high-level wellness and balanced stress.

You do not have to continue the same archaic responses to stress as your prehistoric ancestors did. Our ancestors responded to stress in a fight or flight reaction. This physiological/emotional reaction helped people survive and was effective for that time in history. Today you are reacting to different stresses and demands that force you to make more thoughtful choices. Empowerment allows you to use the marvelous "high tech" that exists within you to make the necessary positive choices and take effective action on them.

Empowerment does not cost . . . it pays!

Empowered individuals receive continuous personal dividends both at home and on the job. Your development into an empowered person will allow you to use more of your talents, strengths, and abilities to handle negative stress. Becoming an empowered person will take concentrated, genuine effort, and work to reach that point, but doing so is worth it. The only costs are efforts while the benefits related to gaining control of your life will pay major dividends.

Life is full of challenges that provide real opportunities for growth. Be thankful for the challenges and the chance you have to use your personal empowerment skills to bust the negative stress in your life. Challenges are gifts to you just the same as are the potentials you possess.

We have tried to present a perspective on personal empowerment along with the tools and information needed to utilize it. Properly used, your improving personal empowerment will help regulate the stress and make life more enjoyable and productive. Life situations and stressors will change but your personal ability to deal with them successfully always can be there for you.

Your empowered approach to the stressors of life and living will separate you from the uninformed and provide feelings of calmness and control. You may not necessarily become financially richer, more powerful, smarter, or more successful because of your personal empowerment (You might though!). No one can predict your future nor guarantee happiness or success. However, the actions you take to make empowerment a way of life are guaranteed to give you more control. You will then be able to congratulate yourself for successes and know that you can make a difference when things go wrong.

Good luck and May The Force of Empowerment Be With You!

REFERENCES

Anderson, R. (1978). *Stress power.* New York: Human Sciences Press.

Benson, H. (1975). *The relaxation response.* New York: Morrow.

Holmes, T. & Rahe, R. (1967). The social readjustment rating scale. *Journal of Psychosomatic Research, 11,* 213-218.

Kobasa, S.C. (1979). Stressful life events, personality, and health: An inquiry into hardiness. *Journal of Personality and Social Psychology, 37,* 1-11.

Lazarus, R. (1966). *Psychological stress and the coping process.* New York: McGraw-Hill.

Monat, A. & Lazarus, R.S. (1977). *Stress and coping: An anthology.* New York: Columbia University Press.

Selye, H. (1956). *The stress of life.* New York: McGraw-Hill.

Selye, H. (1974). *Stress without distress.* Philadelphia: Lippincott.

INDEX

INDEX

ABOUT THE AUTHORS

ABOUT THE AUTHORS

Thomas F. Holcomb is a professor of Guidance and Counseling at Murray State University in Murray, Kentucky. His doctoral degree was earned at the University of Tennessee. He has worked in the area of occupational stress and job burnout through creative self-management approaches for several years. He has been a consultant on stress management to business and industry, human service professionals, school administrators, teachers, and military support personnel. Tom is dedicated to personal empowerment enhancement and believes that developing the skills to manage and cope with stress is a key ingredient of personal power

George John Cheponis is the owner of Growth-Management Consultants in Plymouth, Pennsylvania. He provides keynote addresses, training seminars, consulting, and counseling to government, industry, corrections, health organizations, and education. George has previously worked as a counselor, educator, and program developer for agencies, higher education, and businesses. His doctoral degree was earned at Mississippi State University.

Richard Hazler is a professor of Counselor Education at Ohio University in Athens, Ohio. He did graduate work at Trenton State College, New Jersey, and earned his doctorate at the University of Idaho. Richard has worked as a counselor, trainer, and writer in the Army, a prison, the public schools, and maintains a private practice. He is the author of numerous professional articles on a wide variety of topics, editor of the *Journal of Humanistic Education and Development*, and his latest publication is *The Emerging Professional Counselor* with Jeff Kottler.

Eileen McPhillips Portner is currently Director of a Partial Hospitalization Unit and works in private practice in Allentown, Pennsylvania. She has many years of experience as a professional counselor and trainer in a variety of settings. Her master's degree work was done at Murray State University, Kentucky, and she now holds licenses as a Professional Counselor, Marriage and Family Therapist, and Chemical Dependency Specialist.